## THIS BOOK IS DEDICATED

to my husband, Mickey, and my sister,

Ruthie. You've always seen me with

the eyes of Jesus. You've always been

eager to read or listen to all my words.

I couldn't have done this without you.

# UNADULTERATED

### HIS SCANDALOUS GRACE— YOUR NEW IDENTITY

# ERIN ARRUDA

**BUT JESUS CHRIST** has taken upon himself, by His redemption, to put in me a heart that is so pure that God can see nothing in it to criticize. That is the marvel of the redemption—that Jesus Christ can give me a new heredity, the unsullied heredity of the Holy Spirit. If it is there, Jesus says, his purity will work out in my actual experience.

**Oswald Chambers**
*Studies in the Sermon on the Mount*

## HIS SCANDALOUS GRACE—
## YOUR NEW IDENTITY

# ERIN ARRUDA

Learn more about Erin Arruda and schedule a speaking engagement at her website here: www.erin-arruda.com.

Cover and formatting by Jeff Damm Design, LLC at: www.jeffdammdesign.com

Editing by Lisa Thompson at: www.writebylisa.com. You can email Lisa at: writebylisa@gmail.com

Back cover bio photo by: Jami Guenther

# TABLE OF CONTENTS

# INTRODUCTION

Well, hey, friend. I'm so honored you're here. I imagine you're setting off on a road trip, at a coffee shop, tucked into your bed, or settled into your favorite chair. Wherever you are, you made a conscious decision to use your time—which I know is precious—to read my book. I can't even believe it's really in your hands. Honestly, finishing a book has been a colossal accomplishment, a dream too big for me.

I lived in the same house until I was eighteen. A large framed picture in our home always held a prominent place for us as we grew although it changed rooms from time to time. In it, a little girl looked into a mirror. She had gotten into all her mom's stuff—her jewelry box, shoes, and closet. She was covered from head to toe in an outfit much too big for her. But there she stood, admiring her reflection, even proud of how she looked. Above the picture, this phrase was painted on the glass: "God gives us dreams a size too big so we can grow into them."

Most of my dreams, including this book, feel a size too big. But just like that little girl, I've been invited to try them on by the voice who matters most to me, the Holy Spirit's. I suppose just trying on your dreams, even when or if they don't fit right yet, requires the most faith.

And so, in this written space, as I relive all the places he restored my brokenness with you, I'll be as honest as possible. This means I'll share that through this journey, I have felt like a total mess. I felt and still feel insanely vulnerable. At times, I felt like I couldn't venture here, like I didn't have enough to offer on my own. That's a great place to start. God works best in my emptiness, when I can do nothing but sit there, watching him bring about change in me. In the most vacant places of my soul, he assures me that I am blessed. He whispers, "Erin, my daughter, I am gentle. Trust me.

I am with you. Do not be afraid."

And here, as always, my strength, my resolve, my vision, my passion is restored. I am here with my Jesus, who rescued me, who *always* rescues me. Together, we take another baby step in this vast ocean of love where I see me as he sees me. It's his invitation. It's progress; it's sanctification; it's the process, and it washes over me like calming waves, soothing, with just enough ripple. It offers rest and peace. It reminds me of the beauty of the stillness of my soul. While I know stillness ought to be beneficial and anticipated, the truth is, writing this book was, at times, *painfully* quiet.

The stillness brings order to what was once void. All this stuff that was empty and without form will have a function; it will all take shape; it will be formed—just like the darkness, just like the earth, just like the light. In the stillness comes his voice, saying, "People might theorize and form myths about what I'm creating in you, what I've done for you, and what I've called you out of. But remember, just as I did before, when I separated, formed, and created *e-v-e-r-y-thing*, I am hovering over the waters where you overflow. I am making declarations, separating, and gathering in the darkness to bring light, to give form, removing emptiness by creating something new, by enlarging the capacity of your heart, by filling you up. All that comes first from the stillness, from simply abiding in me. That has taken time for you to learn—twelve years, in fact."

Over the years, while in that place of rest, I became more comfortable with sharing this beautiful story to the point where I just couldn't shut up about it. See, I am too in love with my Savior to not tell you all about what he's done for me, how he's changed me. He is my passionate pursuit. I've discovered in sharing that I'm unable to divulge so many details when I'm limited by a blog or a thirty-minute message. The story of uncovering my identity as a daughter of the King belongs here, in this book. Although it has felt awkward during the process—a size too big—I am growing into it.

Before you dive in, let me explain a few things.

First, I believe that God's love for us is deeply scandalous. Oxford defines scandalous as "causing general public outrage by a perceived offence against morality or law."[1] Yes! That is Jesus. From the day he began his ministry, his grace didn't come in a way that made sense to those who upheld the law. It still doesn't. How can one who offends God with their sin still be worthy to receive his love? Scandalous grace. When we believe and receive it, every impurity is removed from our hearts forever. What was once calloused, dark, and sinful is now completely pure, undefiled, and unadulterated. Unbelievable, isn't it? It doesn't have to be. Stories of scandalous grace are written throughout the pages of the Bible, in the pages of history. The pages of this very book are filled with stories of my own deep experience of his scandalous grace.

Second, the chronology of this book is nearly identical to the way I found my identity in Jesus. He wove the stories of his love from the Bible into my heart, healing my brokenness along the way. The Holy Spirit unlocked the truths and the mysteries of the Word of God. Suddenly, I understood huge theological concepts and passages of Scripture that I had read a hundred times growing up. Even though the Word of God hadn't changed, something in me had. I didn't go to seminary and discover these truths. I learned them the same way Peter did: by spending time with Jesus, by asking questions, by sharing my doubts, and by listening. That is called intimacy.

Friend, we were made for it.

Third, I wrote most of this book in the hills of Tennessee although I'm a Florida girl. I piggybacked on the dreams of someone else—riding fourth wheel with Valley's End, a three-person vocal band, as they recorded their album, *Coming Home*. The band is comprised of my little sister, Ruthie, and two of my dear friends, Pastor Chuck and Pastor Chris. Hearing them sing powerful anthems of praise and restoration provided the perfect background to develop this book. Tears have saturated these words— hope-filled, healing tears. These folks have made me and this book better. So at the start of each chapter, you'll read a glimpse of the words I heard as

I wrote because they bear repeating. They echo what's in my heart.

Fourth, at the end of each chapter, I've included reflection questions. I prayerfully wrote them for you to consider what the Lord wants you to know, uncover, understand, or believe about him. Take your time with them.

Here's one last important point before you dive into this sucker: While I love to write, I'm wired for sit-down, face-to-face dialogue. I want to hear your voice. I want you to see my face, know my tone, and interpret all my body language. I want to have a visual of you. Where are you at? Are you picking up what I'm dropping? I need some affirmation here because I don't want you to miss a thing. I'm wondering if I lost you some place. If you have questions. If something is hard to believe. Penning my story this way required a download of faith that came as I wrote, not a moment too soon. I had to put all those wonderings in Jesus's hands. So I get where you might be at.

Since I prefer an in-house, face-to-face, hand-to-hand-connection while crying and sharing Jesus and a couple cups of coffee together, can we at least try this? Right now, turn this book over so that you have my face in your mind while you read this part.

To you, my friend, I say: Thank you for your time. I will not waste it with words that aren't healing or refreshing to your soul. I saw you in my mind as I wrote. I saw the freedom you seek, that I know firsthand can only come from Jesus. In light of all that, I held nothing back. I bore my soul, both the stuff you might not want to see and the stuff you absolutely have to see. I did this because that's why he gave us each other. It honors him when we have enough courage to share truth with each other with love and grace.

Truly, you should know that I am so much more interested in talking about resurrection than the life and death I left behind. Part of this journey for me has been spent separating myself from that old life. When resurrection came, when forgiveness released me, Jesus built a bridge over the chasm I had created. He invited me to leave the wilderness, the wandering, to join him in the Promised Land. I have spent the last twelve years putting as much space as possible between the real me and that dead carcass I left behind. Going back there seems useless.

Until I think of you.

Some of you are in that wilderness, dying a different kind of death, not the resurrecting kind. I know the feeling well. There's Jesus, though, inviting you to healing, to a new life. He's already built a bridge to the Promised Land, but the chasm is so wide, you're afraid to cross it. And I have a sense that some of you didn't even know there *was* a Promised Land. You think the desert is the only option afforded to you, so you make the best of it. You have determined that you will just create a paradise right there. You find a massive cactus to give you some shade from the scorching sun; you work on your tan, or you build a sand castle. But I'm calling your bluff. I lived there, so I know you are dying in that heat. Don't lie to yourself. There is no relief for your weariness. There is no oasis in this desert, no spring of water, only the mirage of one because you are always thirsty, never satisfied. You need to see that it's a lie as old as those told when the first humans walked on this beautiful earth. And it still works, or you would've already left death and the desert behind. Wilderness warrior, I share this story for you.

# FOREWORD

My friend Erin Arruda is a rare treasure. By that, I don't mean that she has somehow gained access to riches of favor or grace from the Almighty that aren't available for the rest of us. To the contrary, her life shines as a beacon of hope, proving that God adores every single one of us and that his kindness is most evident when we feel least worthy to receive it. Erin is a rare treasure because she has not only allowed God to invade her darkest moments and raise beauty from her ashes, but she has also chosen to share the days she most wants to forget with the entire world because somewhere—right now—a precious son or daughter cannot see a way out of the darkness and needs someone bold enough to shine a light for him or her.

I read the first draft of *Unadulterated* on a flight from Nashville to Tampa, and I cried through every page. And by cried, I don't just mean the cutesy sentimental tears of pride at a friend's significant accomplishment. No. I ugly cried, completely overwhelmed by how our God loves us and how he pursues us until he totally transforms us. I wept as I remembered all the places God has patiently healed me and all the remaining rooms of my heart he stands eagerly waiting for me to let him in.

I wish I could make this required reading for everyone who hungers for God but feels too broken or unworthy for him to intervene in their story. I wish I could put this in the hands of every person who laments over a dead dream or a lifetime of "if onlys" and regrets. I wish every teenager who looks in the mirror and curses what they see would absorb the truths in these pages. I wish every weary perfectionist who feels they will only be enough in God once they do—or undo—enough would pick up this life-changing book.

*Unadulterated* is for all of us who have longed to be loved and who have given our hearts to some other lover, only to find ourselves holding a wreckage of shattered pieces. It is an anthem of hope to tell you that God hasn't left you and he stands eager to heal every broken place. And just like he did with my friend Erin, he is ready to write a new story with you of scandalous, beautiful grace.

Well done, Erin. I see many sons and daughters leaving caves of despair because Christ in you, the hope of glory, showed them the light!

**Chuck Ammons**
*Teaching Pastor*
Overflow Church, Valrico, Florida
Author, *Life in the Overflow*

I KNOW EXACTLY HOW I GOT HERE

CAKED IN MUD

HOW THE MIGHTY FALL.

**"COMING HOME"**

**VALLEY'S END**

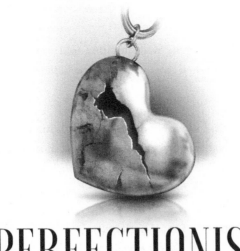

# PERFECTIONISM

**CHAPTER 1**

The heat from the fire intensified, the smoke burning my lungs as I inhaled the black air. I struggled to breathe, desperately trying to salvage my belongings as I rushed through the scorching flames and the billowing smoke. The concentrated heat melted the memories that were displayed all around the life we had created here. I couldn't save them. I couldn't save any of this. Every bit of it was burning and burning rapidly. The darkness and chaos of the engulfing blaze drove me out. So I ran.

Alone, I hustled to a clearing outside the place we lived. The haze of the smoke dissipated at my back. As I turned, the fire disappeared. Instantly. Where everything was once ablaze, only charred rubble remained. It was gone. Completely gone. I stood there in horror, too shocked to breathe, speak, or cry. Then I felt it—something in my hands. *I* have *saved something*, I thought! I looked down. My soot-covered hands held the burnt matches.

Emotionless, the doctor at the walk-in clinic told me what my six other tests confirmed. I sat perched cross-legged on the patient's table as he spoke. "Yes, you're pregnant."

At those fateful words, I saw only destruction. I thought: *You've burned it all down, Erin. Nothing is left. It's charred. And heat is still pulsating from the remains of the marriage you destroyed. People are still devastated. How could you? How did you become this? In four years of marriage, you* never *took a single pregnancy test. You've been on birth control for five years. How is this even possible? You did something wrong. You did many things wrong. You* are *wrong. You've been wrong for so long. You're never going to right this wrong.*

*Just look at him.*

Mickey waited in the companion chair. My attention shifted, and I remembered him. The one I came with. He was there when I heard the words: "Yes, you're pregnant." He was there when the shuddering thoughts came flooding in: *You're a mother. A mother. A baby is growing inside of you at this very second. You are six weeks along. You're sharing your body with another human being. Stop being selfish. Grow up. Go to a real gynecologist. You're almost twenty-eight. How could you not have your life together by now? Get it together. What are you going to do? You're not married. You were, but you burned that down. Remember? Remember how you did that? The affairs. The lies. The cheating. You deserve this, and so does he. Do you even love him? Does he even really love you? How do you know? You've just been having fun. Does he care?*

*Yes.*

*I think.*

*I don't know.*

I searched his face for clues. His demeanor faded from inquisitive, skeptical, and assured to just plain terrified. In a split second, I watched him transform from man/boy to father. I think I even saw his first gray hair grow.

*Did he already hate me for that gray hair? Or for this new title? Does he see these matches in my hand too?*

I couldn't tell you how long that doctor was in the room. I don't know if I asked him a single question. Did the doctor say anything else? I have no idea. My mind was a whirling mess of thoughts. All I could hear were the words in my head that waved the matches in front of my face, taunting me.

This was not the way I imagined bringing a child into this world—into proverbial rubble. I knew this wasn't "right;" that was engrained in me. I couldn't be happy or embrace my beloved in excitement the way I always believed I would when I learned the news of my first pregnancy. Alone, humiliated, ashamed, and hopeless—I had burned down all my dreams and set my life on fire. At this sobering moment, I realized that my world revolved around me. I hated myself more with every rotation.

*Well, how are you going to lie and cheat your way out of this one, Erin? How are you going to cover up this scandal? How are you going to justify your actions this time?*

*I don't know.*

*I don't know.*

*I'm scared.*

*Why did I pick up these matches?*

*How did I get here?*

*What beauty could ever come from these charred remains?*

I stood inside our modest home, holding on to the knob of our front door. Next to me, as near as she could be, was my mother. Her shiny, brown hair brushed against my face as she knelt at the door beside me. Her hand wrapped around mine, soft, firm, and cozy, just like her love. Then and now, she's as gentle and generous as they come. The anticipation of what lie on the other side of that door was palpable to both of us. Her eyes were beaming with an excitement mirrored in mine. None of my siblings were around. This was my own moment. I didn't have to share it or my parents with anyone else. On the other side of that door waited a promise I was certain was just for me. Like a Christmas present, it couldn't be stolen or marked for someone else.

My mom asked, "Erin, are you ready?"

I nodded yes with joy and assurance.

A knock sounded with my Father's voice, low, tender, and familiar. He spoke to me as his child, like he knew I was his but like I was my own person too. I felt independent and wise. It was all so thrilling.

"Erin," he called. "It's Jesus. Can I come into your heart?"

I knew what to do. If the answer was yes, I would simply open the door, which would symbolize my acceptance and belief in the life, death, and resurrection of Jesus. And I *did* believe. I had no doubts. In fact, I had been the one to ask for this moment. I wanted all of Jesus, all of the Jesus I had heard them talk about in their Bible studies, in their worship songs, in our talks at the dinner table, in our prayer times at night, in the stories of restoration I heard in our living room. I believed all of it without hesitation.

So it was an easy choice when my father tenderly beckoned me to recognize

Jesus of my own free will. I turned the knob and pulled the door open with all my might. My mom and dad wrapped their arms around me, rejoicing with me and all the angels in heaven that another one had come to know the love of Jesus Christ.

I was just four years old. Thirty-five years later, I still know and believe that was when I first came to a decision to accept Jesus as my personal Lord and Savior. Though I couldn't articulate all that meant at the time, my heartfelt prayer, "Jesus, come into my heart," was sufficient enough for both of us. Jesus meets us where we are.

Two of my three girls now have similar stories. Both times, my mama just happened to be in our home when they were ready to make those decisions. This time, I was the one next to them by the door, their Daddy on the other side, like a gentleman, waiting, asking, never forcing their acceptance of him and his love. We roared with joy on both occasions, echoing the sounds of heaven.

My parents now boast eleven grandchildren ranging in age from three to twenty-four. We are a big brood with not a shy one in the bunch. Being with them is the happiest place for me. There is no spot I feel more comfortable than with my family, in the middle of loud kids, competitive board games, lots of food, singing songs, and over hearing both silly and deep conversations. The kids create elaborate games, dances, experiments, and treasure hunts. We make room and give time for all of it.

This was how I grew up too. I was the third of four kids. My brother was the oldest, and the three of us girls fell under him. I was in the middle of the three girls, so it felt like I was in the middle of everyone even though, technically, I shared that position with my older sister. I always had someone to play with or talk to.

My parents led several Bible studies, so our home was filled with people for the majority of my childhood. We didn't have much money, and our house was a whopping 1600 sq. ft., with only one bathroom for many years, but our home held so much love. We made room for dancing, singing, playing, wrestling, inventing, imagining, and creating. Love in me grew up here. It was knit into the very fabric of my being. I learned that love looks like spending time together, staying in close proximity, being silly, becoming vulnerable, waiting your turn, and offering and receiving forgiveness. Our home had all that.

This wasn't a perfect or idyllic childhood, make no mistake. But forgiveness built a path over the muddy waters of our many errors.

As a family, we have experienced loss, tragedy, betrayal, and heartbreak. We've suffered. Sometimes it's because of our own stupid decisions. Sometimes it's not. Regardless, it's never a pretty sight when the worst of our stuff is all exposed. It's like mud, when you step in it, it will linger and spread as long as you keep walking. There is no avoiding it. Mud cakes on. Should you attempt to brush it off, you will learn quickly that you've only given it a new place to grow. Literally, I know this to be true.

**This wasn't a perfect or idyllic childhood, make no mistake. But forgiveness built a path over the muddy waters of our many errors.**

I've worked in the real estate industry for the last fifteen years. I've had many victories and experienced lots of defeat during my career, as well as some terribly embarrassing moments. Once I asked a lady when her baby was due. She was very thin and was talking to me about her new baby as if it hadn't arrived yet. Turns out she had already had her baby just *two days* before. Go put your feet up, girl. Why are you here? I'll never know. They didn't buy from me. Go figure.

I did have some other embarrassing moments with better outcomes. Years ago, before kids—when I could wear six-inch heels all day long because my feet, heels, and calves were champions—I met a client at a new construction lot. He was looking for a home in a neighborhood I represented.

On my first step out of the car and onto the lot, I landed in the soft mud. My foot slid down into the earth all the way up to the middle of my shin. I had on my favorite black pants, now drenched in the wet Florida sand. I was still holding on to the car door, thank God, with my other foot firmly planted on the asphalt. I looked at this guy, whom I had never met in person before, in embarrassment and horror. I had no way to get out of this gracefully. I proceeded to gingerly pull out my foot, all the while trying to keep my favorite heel in place. But despite my best efforts, it dislodged half-way out. Once my foot was released, I had to decide whether or not to dive in after the other half of my beloved pair of heels. This poor guy had no idea how to help a woman in this kind of distress. He was in work attire himself and wasn't about to go digging through the mud for my nasty shoe. I was on my own. In one valiant move, I dropped to my knees, centered on the curb, and with one clean arm, retrieved the pump. I shook myself off as best I could.

As we walked across the lot and concrete slab, I continued to attract and release more sandy soil, just like Pigpen from *Charlie Brown*. A cloud of dust swirled around my legs. I went through the motions of walking only to kick up, attach, and shake off more dirt. It didn't stop me. I proceeded to pitch him the lot, muddy hand and foot and all. Unbelievably and in spite of me, he bought it. Maybe it was pity, maybe it was my vulnerability. Either way, a sale is a sale.

This poor client saw me in the muck. I couldn't deny that I was a mess. Truth is, I *hated* that anyone had seen me in such a disastrous state. In your embarrassment or vulnerability, you are hardly thinking, "Gosh, I just can't wait to share this special moment with the world." Right? We crop and edit every ugly thing out of our lives. We only share muddy pictures when we've hilariously failed or when we've come out victorious. Mine is not a story of hilarious failure. It's one of me, deep in the mud, trying to salvage what I lost, brush it off and keep going.

Friend, Jesus took nails in his hands so we wouldn't have to live this life brushing off our muddy mess. He knew this wouldn't be a sufficient ending. He knew, after my sale in the dirt, I would have to go back and face my co-workers. They would all see I was a mess. He knew I would hate their questions and assumptions. He knew I would need a new outfit, picture, and morning.

I haven't always embraced the idea of sharing a picture of me that was less than perfect. In fact, I spent a majority of my teens and twenties covering up, hiding my imperfections, making my life look right, making it *seem* right because I wasn't comfortable with the truth, with the reality, with the muddiness. I didn't want to deal with it or see it. I only showed what I wanted others to see, what I deemed acceptable. Not my real life. I just couldn't. It wasn't what it should be. It didn't seem as good as other people's marriages, jobs, houses, families, GPAs, test scores, credit, bank accounts, lifestyle, talents, artistry, beauty, sense of humor, or just fill in the blank.

Here's proof. I never learned how to do my make up or straighten my hair like most do during adolescence. In high school, I decided to use a razor to trim my crazy bushy eyebrows. You can imagine the outcome. Yep, I ended up shaving half of my left eyebrow off because I didn't know how people actually trimmed or tweezed or waxed their brows. To remedy this very visible eyebrow debacle, I decided to cut my own bangs. Oh, geez. For a chubby girl to give her curly, frizzy hair bangs, when she had no idea what hair straighteners were and YouTube did not yet exist to teach all things, added an incomparable brushstroke to the eyebrow masterpiece I was painting.

Later, my college roommates had this appliance that looked like a flat curling iron. They taught me how to use one on my not-quite-curly, not-

8

quite-straight hair. Bless them, Jesus.

Clearly, I do not have a great track record of fixing my own messes. I'd bet money you don't either. That's why Jesus came. We are messy and broken down until his grace fixes us and cleans us up.

Here's what it looks like. As a mom, this scenario plays out routinely with my three kids. I've become well-practiced at cleaning up messes, especially the ones caked onto those tiny, dirty hands. Not long ago, my daughter and I cringed as we exited the bathroom stall, jazz hands extended, trying to get to the sink and out the door without adding any more germs to our bacteria-laden fingers. She maneuvered her sleeves up just enough and reached for the soap dispenser that I knew was out of her grasp. I intercepted, pumped out the soap, and poured it from my hand into hers.

**Friend, Jesus took nails in his hands so we wouldn't have to live this life brushing off our muddy mess.**

She looked up and said, "Wow, Mom! How did you know I couldn't reach the soap?"

"I just know," I replied.

I just know when my kids are gross and need my help. I just know when their shoes have found the one pile of dog poop that we neglected to find in the backyard that ends up getting tracked into the car or house. *Bleh!* I just know when they haven't washed their hands for dinner or lunch or at all. *Eek!* I just know when they need a morning bath and an evening bath and sometimes one in between. I just know.

What I am realizing more and more is what I just. don't. know. about my own funk.

But that day, as I transferred soap from my hand to my daughter's hand, I caught a glimpse of grace. I saw the Lord's hand instead. And into my hands, he was pouring gobs of gooey, soapy grace. As my girl and I lathered it up and scrubbed it into our fingernails, I saw myself, standing at that sink in my daughter's place. My hands were covered—more than that, my entire body was covered—with dirt and bacteria, sin that was seen and unseen, obvious and microscopic. There I stood, covered in selfishness and pride, anxiety and jealousy, doubt and fear, and so much more.

It wasn't the cringe-worthy stuff I knew I had done that came as a surprise. It was the other smelly messes I had somehow stepped in along the way that were overwhelming to see. Somehow, somewhere, I had walked right into a pile of sin, just like that mud, and it was stuck to the bottom of my shoe, and I was tracking it everywhere with me. It was stinking up my home, my kids and husband, friends, church, plus anybody and everybody I ran into along the way. Steaming piles of selfishness, pride, fear, and the like—yeah, those have a way of leaving an impression wherever you go. They tend to really stink up a place.

**For a long time, truthfully, I couldn't bear the idea of knowing that my sin would contribute to the death that delivered the very grace and forgiveness I needed.**

Before I could tread one more nasty step, I was intercepted by his cleansing, amazing grace. It was an endless supply! And to that soapy grace, he added his aroma of forgiveness, peace, and wisdom.

His kind of forgiveness says, "I'm not going to hold that nastiness against you ever again. You're clean. You're beautiful. I still like you. I still love you. I still accept you."

His kind of peace says, "I knew you couldn't reach, and no matter how much you grow, you will never reach it without me. I'm the soap dispenser. I'm the grace giver. Get off your tippy toes, stop straining, and just receive what I am pouring out."

His kind of wisdom says, "Let me walk with you. I know which direction you should go, so ask me. I would love to help you avoid the muck and mire."

When we come face to face with his grace, we sometimes feel unworthy to receive it. For a long time, truthfully, I couldn't bear the idea of knowing that my sin would contribute to the death that delivered the very grace and forgiveness I needed. I thought I could do it on my own. That I could somehow earn his promises for me.

Parents and children alike, please know this: *That's the scheme! That's the assignment!* The enemy wants to bury the kids of Christian families under the subtle lie of perfectionism. Identity theft is not a new concept. It's at the start of the story of mankind. Parents and churches might not intend to burden their children with these requirements, but their own lists of dos and don'ts can still create bondage. Don't eat that. Don't touch that. Do it right. Be good. Get it done. Read more. Quiet down. Go on a mission trip. Raise your hands. Sing the songs. Sing them louder. Don't drink. Don't smoke. Don't cuss. Close your eyes. Bow your heads. Fold your hands. Say Amen. Smile even when you don't feel like it . . . or you surely will die.

It's legalism. It's perfectionism. It's religion.

Those are the sins that bound me in my youth. Like a pendulum, I swung between thinking I could never be perfect to believing I should try to be perfect. And what I really believed is that I could do it if I just. worked. harder.

Perfectionism breeds in us the fear of failure. In both legalism and perfectionism, we can see such a deep desire to succeed that we are willing to be godless to gain any amount of it. There is no room for grace in the walls of these two *isms*.

As I grew up, my family didn't put these expectations on me. But I still had lots of unanswered questions about these do's and don'ts. I just didn't ask them. And when we fail to ask and fail to seek the truth, we can leave room for the enemy to deceive us. As many of us do as young adults, I began to exchange those truths for what I could reason, justify, or earn. It's so much easier to do that. Somewhere along the way, I had decided that I loved Jesus too much to be the reason that he suffered and died. I couldn't accept his free gift. I couldn't accept that Jesus should die for me. In doing so, I robbed the cross of his death for me. And since I couldn't let him die for me, I certainly couldn't walk in resurrected life with him. My own pride left me unable to surrender my life.

**On August 26, 2013, I journaled this:**

*Tonight I saw myself at such a young age. The vows I made to myself— that I wouldn't try unless I knew I could succeed—are silly. I did such a thing because of how I felt about others seeing me. Really all that matters is my worship unto you.*

I understand now, with Jesus, I am made perfect! If we are struggling with perfectionism for ourselves or others, then how can we celebrate the grace we've found? Where can it possibly have room to grow? How can it seep into others? Our forgetfulness, our human weakness, our misunderstandings, and ineptitude can be welcomed through the eyes of grace, perfecting us through the precious blood of Jesus.

The Christian life becomes a burdensome list if it's not fueled by the love and worship of our Father and King. Lists and obligations have no residence in our created identity. We'll never experience freedom in shoulda, woulda, or coulda. Those doubts just cause regret. Doubt is such a bugger. It's not wrong to doubt. In fact, Jesus is begging us to bring him our doubts. He wants to shower us with truth and is not insecure in the least. Our doubts are an indication of our honest hearts, which he longs for us to share so that he can encourage us to believe. Otherwise, those doubts fester and turn into unbelief, which steals our hope. Now we're in some trouble.

After Jesus died, was buried, and rose again, Thomas had some doubts and wanted to see Jesus for himself, to feel the places where those nails had pierced his hands. He was struggling to believe what others were telling him. Jesus gave such grace to Thomas, imploring him, "'Put your finger here, and look at my hands. Put your hand into the wound in my side. Don't be faithless any longer. Believe!'" (John 20:27).

Seeing his grace unfold like that helped me realize how much time I wasted living a life of appearances. All that hiding snowballed. I lied so much to myself and others that eventually, all that I was protecting and shielding by way of my deception was exposed. I lost everything: tangible things, yes; relationships, yes; myself, yes; and my faith, well, I was barely holding on to the very last thread.

Jesus shares a parable known to many as the parable of the prodigal son (Luke 15:11–32). A man had *two* sons and one of them, greedy to sow his wild oats, begged for his inheritance from his father before the appointed time. The father released his inheritance to him. With that, the son left his father's home, squandering the money on prostitutes and recklessness. Once his money was gone, he found himself destitute, ashamed, and desperate. He took a job feeding pigs. He was so hungry, he ended up eating the slop he was doling out for the swine. He realized his father never treated his employees that way. They always had enough and never lacked anything. So he decided to humble himself, go home to his father, and repent. Perhaps, he thought, his father would at least allow him to return as an employee.

Upon seeing his son in the distance, the father ran to him, rejoiced, pulled out his best garments, and threw an epic bash. With open arms, he welcomed his repentant son home, embracing him though he smelled like a pig and looked like a beggar.

I always thought that was a sweet story growing up, but if I'm being honest, the second son's perspective resonated more with me than the first son's. See, the other son always did what he was supposed to do. This son worked hard to make his father proud. Even when the prodigal was partying, the second son was working in the field. The older brother refused to celebrate his baby brother's return. He's irate with his dad, asking, "How many years have I been working like a slave for you, performing every duty you've asked as a faithful son? And I've never once disobeyed you. But you've never thrown a party because of my faithfulness."

Have you ever felt like that? See, all the faithfulness of the older son masquerades as righteousness, but it's really self-righteousness. It seems innocent and godly, but it reeks of pride and leads—at least for me—to perfectionism, measuring sin, and earning love. It turned ugly as you can imagine. We only let a select few, if anyone at all, see our muddy shoes, because it requires vulnerability. It's so easy to show a pretense of reality without actually being real nowadays. We can delete, crop, add a filter or a funny caption, or take a hundred shots to capture the perfect selfie. These actions aren't sinful in and of themselves, but we have to be cautious about the snare of perfectionism.

I like a tidy home. There isn't anything wrong with that unless it becomes my identity, unless I can't be joyful in a mess. I like to wear make-up. I like to spruce up the house, redecorate a room, paint, and make it all homey. That's not a problem. Unless I can't leave the house without make-up. Unless I won't let anyone into my house in the middle of a project. Unless I don't let anybody see me in the ugly. Filters and editing features aren't the problem. The issue is that often the perfect picture we display can isolate us and hide the reality that we are circling destruction spiritually, emotionally, and/or physically, which is just what happened to the firstborn prodigal.

**You can only sustain that life for so long because—as the father of the prodigal points out—slavery is not your inheritance.**

The ugliness and imperfections, those are things we dare not confront: the reality of our kids' messy behavior, our struggling marriage, our empty bank account, our distant relationship with God, our vain obsession with beauty, our inflated job status, our devastating failures, our epic disappointments, our fear of intimacy, our fear of losing control, and our unworthiness. These things will steal your identity and hold it hostage until you choose to confront them with the help of the Holy Spirit.

The reply of the firstborn prodigal's father echoes the Father's reply to us. "Child, everything I have is yours to enjoy."

That young man missed it just as we miss it. He didn't find joy in the faithfulness. He didn't think he had any true inheritance of love. Because of that, he couldn't serve from a heart that says, "I love you." He did it from a heart that first wonders, "Do you love me?" and then surmises, "Since I'm not certain of your love, I'll do my best to give you every reason to love me. I'll work so hard for your love, to pay it back, to earn it. I won't work like a servant; I'll work like a slave."

You can only sustain that life for so long because—as the father of the prodigal points out—slavery is not your inheritance. Jesus is clear that as his followers, our lives are meant to look *more* than extraordinary. A life lived from understanding your identity as a child of God with the blessing of his inheritance needs no editing or cropping or filters. The whole picture, messy and muddy as it might have been, is now unbelievably beautiful because Jesus ran it through his filter of grace. The former sins of my life haven't changed. They're still as ugly as they ever were, but now, they are covered with God's redemption. I see *him*, not me, when I reflect on my past.

Friends, in case you didn't see it yet, there were *two* prodigals in this story. Let me tell ya, I have lived both lives. Neither is better than the other. One makes you a slave to perfectionism; one, a slave to temptation. They are both ill-fated destinies.

## LET'S REFLECT:

Has perfectionism been a struggle for you? How? If you aren't sure, look back at some of the thoughts on perfectionism in this chapter.

Who do you identify with more: the prodigal who left or the prodigal who stayed?

As a believer, do you believe that your inheritance is an extraordinary life lived with Jesus and loved by him?

Where has doubt, even the tiniest bit, caused unbelief about God's true character and what he longs to give you?

What are you trying to keep hidden from Jesus?

What is your true identity and inheritance? Grab a blank sheet of paper and fill it with a picture or words of how the Father sees you and the inheritance and plans he has for you.

TIMING IS EVERYTHING.

**MY DAD**

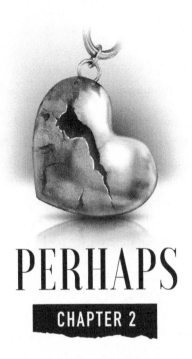

# PERHAPS

**CHAPTER 2**

I stood there in my pristine white, beaded wedding dress. One hand held onto a bouquet of pink gerbera daisies; the other clenched my father's arm. The arch in the garden under the old, live oak tree was sprinkled perfectly with flowers. The day was not as hot as expected for the end of May in Florida. Everything was prepared. Everyone was in place. Everyone knew their cues.

Except me.

The bridesmaids and groomsmen were lined up in a clearing ahead of me. As the string quartet started playing, my father and I stepped out to walk from behind the azaleas to the white runner that lined my path and covered the earth. On the tip of my tongue were the words, "I think this is a mistake."

Anticipating my destiny, I turned to speak what was in my heart. Anticipating my destiny, my father's eyes teared up. He was so proud to walk me down the aisle. The pride shining in his eyes as he escorted me made me feel so honored. I love this man, my father. Those were the easy words. The others, mentioning my mistakes, they were impossible to say.

Taking our first steps toward the white aisle, I looked up and saw the bridal party filing into the clearing just as we had practiced. We were about to be cut off by the entourage when I realized we had walked out to the wrong music. It wasn't my turn yet. And so with that misstep, my courage, along with the opportunity to speak those words of regret, evaporated. I pulled on my father's arm and in the most ironic and honest moment of my life, I simply said, "Daddy, it's not time yet."

We backed up to resume our places as I tried to compensate for poor timing. As I waited, shrugging off my mistake, all the "How did I get heres?" flooded my mind. I couldn't analyze those nagging questions at that moment, so I pushed them to the side. When the right note hit, I moved forward, marching toward the front, toward the promise. My promise to have and to hold wasn't as much of a concern for me as public shame and embarrassment. I couldn't fathom the idea of telling everyone that I was having second thoughts. Those are normal, right?

Growing up, my love for Jesus was real. I knew him. He talked to me. Words were spoken over me that I know were directly from him. These have made eternal deposits in my soul. Promises were spoken, and vows were made between us. My parents received vows and promises about me and for me too. I studied his Word; I led Bible studies; I worshipped with abandon; I served others out of my love for him and his many children, and my heart constantly cried out for more of him.

I knew and still know that he holds many promises for me. One of those promises I clung to from an early age was my desire to be married and have a family. I knew he had set apart someone just for me. I'm not about to say that I believe this promise is for everyone. I just knew it was for me. My mom spent many years praying for my spouse because she knew that the time she spent with my husband and I would far exceed the time she spent with me alone. Who I married was vitally important to how I would operate as a daughter of the King. So she spent many hours praying for the spouses of each of her four kids.

On occasion, when it was fitting, she would share what the Lord revealed to her about our spouses. Generally, it wasn't anything of great significance. She was just doing her thing, faithfully sowing seeds of prayer. Diligence and faithfulness brings the greatest harvest. That's what my mom did and still does: She intercedes for her biological and spiritual children, and the harvest of goodness is vast because of it.

By middle school—prime boy-crazy age—many of my friends were already making out in the backs of cars. I'd hear them talk about it at the bus stop. They shared how in love they were with a boy, and ultimately the "he said, she said" drama would ensue. I got all wrapped up in their joys and pains of boyfriends at eleven, twelve, and thirteen. I listened expectantly and with a twinge of jealousy, desperate to have a story like theirs. Even then, I was clinging to the promise and hope that love would find me, when I, too, would make out in the back of a car with a boy. But godly ideals were even wrapped up in those thoughts because I wanted to honor the Lord with my body and my life. My version of the story would be different because I was, after all, a good girl.

I dreamed that we would be older and he would be my husband—who had a firm foundation of faith, who loved me, who wanted to spend the rest of his life with me, and who loved Jesus even more than he loved me! You guys, I was all in with my vows of "true love waits", with my promise ring attached firmly to the fourth finger of my left hand.

During that time, I asked my mom about my husband. I was clinging to hope and desperately seeking another little piece of the promise. I wondered, was God's promise for me still true? Could it be that God had someone special in mind for me? That day, while in the throes of middle-school drama, she told me that she had been praying for my husband, and

God revealed that in between middle school and high school, he would go through something very tragic, but God would have his hand on this young man and be near to him. I asked her no less than a thousand more questions. Her only response was for me to pray for him. I did.

> Like many young women, I was eager for the promises of love and devotion, so I disregarded the checks in my spirit.

Does this seem crazy? Yes. I get that. Listen, if I wasn't standing on the other side of the truth, I might think this was irrational, blurry, and a figment of my imagination. But when I was growing up, I thought it was completely normal and miraculous. I loved being reminded of God's promises for me. I knew that included a husband and children. Every time my mom prayed for him or revealed something from the Holy Spirit about him, I came into agreement with the promise again and sometimes innocently added a bit of my own plot lines to the story. As we sometimes do, I put my own desires on the throne of my heart instead of God's desires for me.

I was so impatient for love, so terrified of being alone, that I ignored the red flags God sent as my first serious relationship progressed in my early twenties. Our dating, including our engagement, lasted a year and a half. Two months of that time I spent backpacking through Europe with my dear friend. I should've known then that absence should make the heart grow fonder. But even in the new, early stages of love, my eyes were already wandering. I should have realized that something wasn't right and heeded that warning right from the start. Even then, perfectionism was rearing its ugly head. Like many young women, I was eager for the promises of love and devotion, so I disregarded the checks in my spirit. You know, those uneasy feelings you get. Those warnings in hindsight seemed so loud and obvious, but in the midst of trying to maintain a pretense of control over my future, they seemed like white noise, unworthy of attention.

Dr. John Van Epp, a clinical psychologist, has researched and developed many programs regarding love and relationships. I learned about him a little too late to keep me from some of the trouble I would find myself in, but I wanted to introduce some of his research here early on in this story, where I wish I would've learned it. It's called the Relationship Attachment Model (RAM).[2] He uncovers five foundations to build on as a relationship progresses: know, trust, rely, commit, touch. He encourages people to follow this order in a relationship so that the relationship does not become imbalanced.

I didn't do that. I rushed in. In most of my relationships these principles were introduced backwards of the model.

Just one month after I got home from Europe, 9/11 occurred. Even though the terrorism was over a thousand miles away, I felt small, afraid, confused, and alone. I was a senior in college. The tumultuous world, non-existent jobs, and an unknown future seemed too close for my comfort. Two weeks later, with my thoughts still reeling, with questions still hanging unanswered, he asked me to marry him. Grasping for some sense of stability in such an uncertain world, I said, "yes," promising an unknown future to this willing partner. I was hedging my bets that all the promises the Lord had given me, all the dreams I held about my future as a wife and a mom, would begin and end with this man. Only at that age (twenty-two), I didn't take it quite as seriously as I should have. I didn't consider the cost before buying the field as Jesus advises in his wise words.

I was guilty that day of picking up a promise that didn't belong to me and surrendering a promise that *did* belong to me, to someone besides Jesus, a new husband. Picking up promises that have been wrapped and tagged for someone else always has consequences. We do that so innocently. Most of us aren't malicious in our intent. At that young age, what did I know yet of such lasting consequences? What did I understand yet of blessings and curses?

I would learn later of the story in Genesis 15 that would bring me freedom from my broken promises and rerouted plans. It brought healing and understanding to my human condition known as forgetfulness.

Here in this first book of the Bible, we find God coming to Abraham in a vision. The Lord tells him not to be afraid, that God is his protection and his great reward. But Abraham is lamenting. His heart is aching, which is keeping him from trusting God. He wants a child, an heir, a future, and a legacy. He is an old man with a large inheritance. So he asked God if he should leave his inheritance to his servant.

In those days, the master could adopt the son of a trusted servant and leave the inheritance to him. When Abraham asked if he could or should entrust the value of his family legacy into the hands of one who was not his biological heir, God said, "no," and told him this:

"This man will not be your heir, but a son who is your own flesh and blood will be your heir." He took him outside and said, 'Look up at the sky and count the stars—if indeed you can count them.' Then he said to him, 'So shall your offspring be'" (Genesis 15:4–5, NIV).

The blessing God was bestowing on Abraham was given to him because of his faith in the Lord and his obedience to him. It was considered righteousness, a right way of living and abiding in Yahweh. God called him righteous as a result of his belief that God would do what he said he would do: make Abraham the father of a nation.

After that, God made a great display of favor and love toward Abraham. He blessed the land he would inherit and made a covenant with him. In that divine exchange, Abraham heard the promise of God in the King's Valley. Kind of a fitting name, huh? The promise for heirs as numerous as the stars, for the choicest land, for peace in death, and for favor over his enemies. And yet we find Abraham forgetting all that just a few verses later. Or perhaps, he was just confused on how to get to the end promise, losing patience, and not consulting God on the best route to take. Hmm. . . sounds familiar.

Enter Abraham's wife, Sarah, who says to Abraham, "The Lord has kept me from having children. Go, sleep with my slave [servant]; *perhaps* I can build a family through her" (Genesis 16:2, NIV, emphasis added).

Abraham, who had just been in the presence of God, who had just been given a lasting covenant as the father of all nations, who had joined in agreement with God's promises, didn't protest her reasoning or desire.

Baffling, this human condition. What seems so clear one moment is completely forgotten later. Why do we encounter a true, honest, and empowering moment with God and then forget to ask him for his counsel when temptation arises?

The word perhaps weaves its way into those desires, into our logic. It's not a very commanding word. It's simply an idea, a suggestion, an opportunity. These words— idea, suggestion, opportunity—they don't seem that threatening. But oh, that word perhaps as it relates to obedience to God's plan has gotten me into a lot of trouble.

*Perhaps* this is what God meant when he said . . . .

*Perhaps* this is the way God wants me to go . . . .

*Perhaps* he is using this to . . . .

*Perhaps* you should . . . .

*Perhaps* he's the one . . . .

And just like that little word does for us, perhaps got the better of Abraham and Sarah, even though Abraham had just witnessed God's power, promise, and faithfulness.

I wonder what he must've felt like when Sarah told him to go ahead and sleep with her maidservant. Her heart must've truly been broken, awaiting God's promises. Her patience had worn thin. See, Abraham had seen the fire of the Lord; he had seen him walk through the sacrificed animals to symbolize their covenant. But she had only a second-hand knowledge of God's promises. The promises were intended for her as well, but she didn't come into full agreement with what was hers. She didn't believe in faith. She didn't rest on God's word. We're not mad at you, Sarah. Are we? No way! Because we still do the same thing!

A whole book of promises is sitting in front of me right now. When I read them, I'm receiving second-hand knowledge, but I'm still a full portion-bearer. Get that? That's how God works as our provider. The blessing is the same for the first generation as it is for a thousand generations to those who love him; yet I fail to receive them, own them, walk in them. (See Exodus 20:6 and Deuteronomy 5:10). These blessings include: honor, power, revelation, faith, righteousness, eternity, goodness, mercy, protection, favor, healing, fruitfulness, hope, love, and a thousand more, and I constantly fail to take hold of them.

I believe in perhaps instead of a promise. I come into agreement instead with what I can see with my earthly eyes. Me of little faith.

"By faith we understand that the universe was formed at God's command, so that what is seen was not made out of what was visible" (Hebrews 11:3, NIV).

Let me tell you: there is no confident hope; there is no faith in *perhaps*. When you're walking in uncharted waters with the Lord, is your faith emboldened or wavering? For me, it's a bit of both. When we feel uncertain, we need to hold fast to faith. Our beautiful sister Sarah wasn't exactly living in that place. She wasn't living by faith. She couldn't see what would come from what wasn't yet visible. Instead, she saw her wrinkled hands, her aging body, her gray and thinning hair. Instead of clinging more tightly to the unseen promise, she relied on what was pressing in around her: physical impossibilities, barrenness, and death. Sarah was hedging her bets on building the family God had promised her through her own will and way, through Hagar, someone other than the Great I AM.

When I think about her story, I have to suspect that she loved Hagar. I imagine you wouldn't invite a woman to sleep with your husband unless you respected her, unless she was humble, right? I mean, the idea is so far outside of our thinking

**This is our human forgetfulness, the weakness and frailty of our minds. The places that must be submitted to the Holy Spirit lest we conceive perhaps children.**

today that we imagine she either didn't love her husband much, didn't respect him, or didn't believe that God's hand was upon her.

I think it's the latter. It's almost always the latter.

Me and my girl, Sarah, had a lot to learn. We had to grow up in our faith a little . . . errrrr—a lot. See, somewhere during that time of hope deferred, Sarah grew tired of waiting. And somewhere during that time between the dreams of adolescence and the reality of adulthood, so did I. I started looking at the throne where God's promises resided. I began to grow impatient that he hadn't handed them to me yet, so I coated his promises with perhaps-ism (doubt) and legalism (control).

Sarah started looking at her maidservant and acted in accordance with her own will, seeking to manage the situation. She had separated herself from the guiding patience of the Holy Spirit and sided with control, outsourced through a hurried response. This is our human forgetfulness, the weakness and frailty of our minds. The places that must be submitted to the Holy

Spirit lest we conceive *perhaps* children. Then little by little, we exchange each of those heavenly promises, blessings, and desires for pleasures of the flesh.

Perhaps created an environment that meant every time I found someone that might, could, possibly love me, I lost myself, my hope, patience, and promise. I moved the person onto the throne only intended for the one true God, and I expected him to fulfill the promise. It brought heartbreak every time. I lamented my decision, and each time, I gave in to sexual temptation. I concocted the mixture of doubt and control and buried the promise that this boy that I was physically and emotionally giving my heart and body to would be my husband—who had a firm foundation of faith, who loved me, who wanted to spend the rest of his life with me, and who loved Jesus even more than he loved me. I lamented and buried. Why? Because we forget. And when we are tempted, we can easily exchange every bit of God-breathed boundary and desire for righteousness for a desire for pleasure, hoping that the rest of the things will be added. We tear godly promises down one layer at a time until all we have left is a desire to make out—or more—in the car, because we think it will lead to the one thing our hearts are really after: love. It's a perhaps mentality that robs God of his throne and steals our promises.

Exchanging promises and purpose for "perhaps, I . . . " is an illusion of control. I bought and exchanged my innocence for this lie, just like Sarah did. "Perhaps, *I* can build a family through *her*" (Genesis 16:2, NIV, emphasis added.) When we write it out like that, we see it plainly, don't we? We're saying, "I've got this. I can build it. I can find another way, perhaps even a quicker route with less suffering."

What I've learned by now is that when we pray for God's kingdom to come and reign in our situation, and it doesn't happen the way we envisioned it, we try to create the kingdom ourselves. We start constructing towers around God's usurped throne, which we hope will fit in God's plans, none of which are actually a part of his architectural designs.

Friends, let's learn this lesson for the last time. Let's listen to wisdom that is yelling in the streets. (See Proverbs 1:20.) If it's constructed by our own hands, we have to be prepared to construct it with our own resources and maintain it with our own strength. Spoiler alert: We are not made for that kind of burden. It will bankrupt and crumble us every time. Because we exchange godliness for pleasure, for our own plan, at great loss to ourselves.

John 12:24 tells us that a grain of wheat will remain a grain of wheat unless it is buried in the earth and dies. Only then can it produce a harvest. Jesus explains this parable to be sure we don't misunderstand how to enter the kingdom of heaven or what's valuable in the kingdom of God. The person who caters to his own will, who pampers his own life, will miss real life offered through Jesus Christ. Life will *feel* empty because it will *be* empty. This kind of life bears no lasting fruit. If I want him to work in me, then I must be empty of myself, laying all my best tools and tricks at his feet. I must come impoverished and dead to my own ways in order for his ways to come alive in me, in order to walk in resurrection, in the new way.

I've read a lot of books about how the Lord has redeemed people from traumatic situations: life-changing stories of death, destruction, disease, trauma, brokenness, and evil. In this story of me and my redemption through Jesus Christ, you'll see how I created the trauma, the brokenness, the evil, and the destruction. I did it by my own hand, through my own sin, just like so many of my friends in the Bible. We have moved ourselves out of purpose, grace, and promise and chosen to build our own castles. Here's the problem: when we trap ourselves in a perhaps mentality—and oh, goodness, aren't we so good at this?—we face serious consequences. Sarah and I eventually gained a new perspective but not without heartbreak, pain, humiliation, and fear. But what we fail to remember and what we'll talk about later is after the consequences for both me and my Bible friend, Sarah, the forgiveness, the humility, and the surrender comes. It kills the fertilizers of doubt and control. It pours on the waters of hope and grows the buried promises—those grains of wheat we all think are dead. And in

God's perfect timing, what was buried comes to life in good soil—better, perhaps—because of the poop we've added that's been rotated through it.

I love Sarah. I so get her. I wasn't yet clinging to the truths I know now. Neither was she. The land seemed barren. My world seemed barren. Death seemed more imminent than life. I know what it feels like to see my circumstances obscure the promise. I had prayed for his kingdom to come so many times. I had prayed for him to answer my prayers so many times. I had prayed for real love so many times. And let me tell you, he brought the kingdom down every. single. time. I just didn't come into agreement with it because it looked more like spending time with Jesus rather than spending time with a cute guy that perhaps, loved Jesus. That didn't seem like as much fun on a Saturday night. That's because I didn't know him then like I know him now.

Giving up pieces of the promise, siding with fear instead of faith, was easier. I buried patience. I buried promise. The stage was set for me to meet my first husband. One day while at work, I looked at the guy who had been staring at me from across the bar for a while, and said to myself, "Perhaps." From there, I started building a family through him. I opened the door for temptation.

## LET'S REFLECT:

Where have you welcomed a *perhaps* scenario into your life that has distracted you from God's original design for you?

I put my first husband on the throne of my heart. Have you ever done this with another person?

In what ways have you constructed your dreams with your own hands without surrendering them first to the Inscriber of your dreams?

Where are your dreams crumbling or becoming difficult to sustain?

What is God inviting you to do with them?

Are there promises that you believed as a child that you're too afraid to believe for now? Can you believe that God will resurrect them?

AND I WILL NEVER UNEARTH A TREASURE

OR ONE SINGLE PLEASURE

THAT DOESN'T COME FROM YOUR HAND

APART FROM YOU, I HAVE NO GOOD THING.

**"PSALM 16"**

**VALLEY'S END**

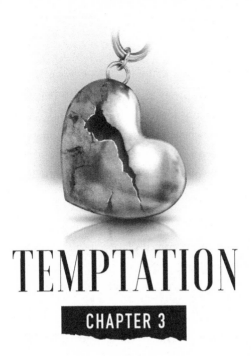

# TEMPTATION

## CHAPTER 3

In the masterful satire, *The Screwtape Letters* by C.S. Lewis, a demon named Screwtape is sending instructional letters to a less experienced demon, his nephew. The nephew's assignment is to torment and distract his patient, a human. "The Enemy" in this story is God, and "Our Father" is really our enemy, Satan. This fictitious account is a wise parable of the demise of our humanness as it relates to our failures to submit our deepest dreams, fears, doubts, and heartaches before an all-powerful God. This comes through humility. When we don't bend toward surrender, then we err toward, among many things: pleasure, intellect, lust, comfortability, and vanity:

> You must therefore conceal from the patient the true end of Humility. Let him think of it not as self-forgetfulness but as a certain kind of opinion (namely, a low opinion) of his own talents and character. Some talents (I gather) he really has. The great thing is to make him value an opinion for some quality other than truth, thus introducing an element of dishonesty and make-believe into the heart of what otherwise threatens to become virtue. By this

method, thousands of humans have been brought to think that humility means pretty women trying to believe they are ugly and clever men trying to believe they are fools. And since what they are trying to believe may, in some cases, manifest nonsense, they cannot succeed in believing it, and we have the chance of keeping their minds endlessly revolving on themselves in an effort to achieve the impossible.[3]

That's how lies work. They're small, stealing a word here or there, developing inference in unnoticed places, sneaking up on you like a snake. We'll develop this next part of the story of this old life I once lived, staring into the beady, dubious eyes of the snake, the father of lies.

In my earliest years and on into middle school, my parents were new in their faith, uncovering the riches of the treasure they had found. They were eager and ready to share with everyone. That's how I came to know Jesus. Their faithfulness to his enduring love fueled their faithfulness to a community of people desperate for peace. I saw it all. It was so real and pure and attractive to me that I didn't feel as if I'd ever need anything else. But so often, we don't know what we don't know. And when we can't explain the truth of God, how can we expect the generation before us to come into agreement with it, especially as logic and reason develop and they begin to question truth during adolescence?

These are impressionable ages. Young people are embarking on quests for truth, and we cannot be afraid of their questions. They are the Google and the YouTube generation. Conviction of truth and genuine connection poured into the life of a young person create a strong foundation for a sold-out believer. Young people can find answers anywhere; what they can't find is connection.

At a very key time in my teenage years, as I began to question my values, my parents were going through their own crisis of faith that I couldn't understand. As a result, they stopped going to church for a while.

My little sister and I had several friends in a youth group together, and we began attending with them each week. This meant, on Sunday nights, we would all pile into the Johnson family home. Bill and Donna welcomed each one of us. Their house was small, but their love for the next generation was immense. We filled their home weekly as we all crammed into every couch, cushion, and crevice. With great love, they played music, listened to our endless stories, and fed us whatever was available in their kitchen. They never once kicked us out.

When they took us to summer camp, my best friend was moving out of the country. They marked the occasion by letting us take over devotions, cry, and sing "Friends Are Friends Forever" in the cabin to the rest of the campers. I'll never forget it. I don't remember what every devotion or message was about, but I remember that love was expressed every time we met with them. I can still feel the truth of the love gospel in my bones. They gave all that they had because their love for Jesus was such that it couldn't be contained to just each other; it had to reach beyond themselves.

They stood in the gap when my parents were unable to do so. They brought no judgement toward my parents; they didn't condemn them or refute them, ever. For us, they simply offered attention and counsel at a time when I wasn't receiving much at home. I truly believe, because of that, my sister and I stayed the course in our faith through middle and high school. We leaned toward heaven instead of the world.

My parent's hiatus from church left a mark in my heart. It would be many years before I could go to them for counsel. As my parents worked out their own faith, I found myself coming to their bedroom door, eager to ask questions about the world, my home, my friends, and my feelings that I couldn't understand. The more I attempted to enter, the more I felt as if I were a burden. I was another thing they had to work through. Eventually, I stopped approaching their door. I no longer felt welcome there. My presence seemed like an interruption or even, at times, created conflict.

They weren't in the right frame of mind to welcome discussion. And I forgive and release them for the pain, confusion, and rejection I felt then.

When I began to create paths of perhaps instead of purpose and promise, I fully withdrew from the wisdom and guidance of my parents. My decision was not without consequences: I created a divide with my sin. I thought their way was theirs. I decided to find my own way, which would be easier and better. It wouldn't include attending weekly church services because "Jesus is wherever I am." I no longer believed in the communion of saints in a building or the ordained leadership of a pastor. I had no need for it. I was part of a new generation comprised of a love religion instead of an organized one, never thinking the two could or should intersect. Before I even knew what it was, I had joined the group of "dones" who no longer attended church.

> **I was part of a new generation comprised of a love religion instead of an organized one, never thinking the two could or should intersect.**

As I moved out of youth group and into my college years, I struggled to find a place I belonged. I was out of the teenage years which hold, so many of us assume, the greatest temptation and identity struggles. But temptation is not limited to a certain age or a certain person. Temptation comes to all of us at any time. No one is immune. Jesus faced forty intense days of temptation and testing in his thirties, right before he walked into his full ministry partnership here on earth as a human. He had also just received the baptism of the Holy Spirit. If Jesus faced this kind of intense temptation in his thirties, why are we surprised when it comes to strong believers? This has been his tactic from the first pages of your Bible, where we find an enemy sliding himself into the garden, into our story.

In the early chapters of Genesis, the Bible tells us that the serpent was more skilled in deceit than any living creature. Manipulatively, this serpent (Satan) comes to the woman and says: "Can it really be that God has said, 'You shall not eat from the trees of the garden?'" Genesis 3:2–7 puts it as follows:

> And the woman said to the serpent, "We may eat fruit from the trees of the garden, except the fruit from the tree which is in the middle of the garden. God said, 'You shall not eat from it nor touch it, otherwise you will die.'" But the serpent said to the woman, "You certainly will not die! For God knows that on the day you eat from it your eyes will be opened [that is, you will have greater awareness], and you will be like God, knowing [the difference between] good and evil." And when the woman saw that the tree was good for food, and that it was delightful to look at, and a tree to be desired in order to make one wise and insightful, she took some of its fruit and ate it; and she also gave some to her husband with her, and he ate. Then the eyes of the two of them were opened [that is, their awareness increased], and they knew that they were naked; and they fastened fig leaves together and made themselves coverings (author's paraphrase).

The Almighty Creator put two beautiful fruit-filled trees in the middle of the garden. One was the tree of life; one, the tree of the knowledge of good and evil. When Adam and Eve listened to the serpent, they forgot God's full command, "You are *free* to eat from any tree in the garden; but you must not eat from the tree of the knowledge of good and evil, for when you eat from it you will certainly die" (Genesis 2:16b–17, emphasis added). They were free to make a choice. Our Father champions the cause of freedom for us. He withholds nothing. He always, always places before us life and death, blessings and curses, the law of love and the law of sin. He doesn't hide anything. He doesn't sugarcoat the sin and curse. There is no trickery or deception. He tells us the truth about it. He is commanding us to not eat from it because it is poison to us and to our relationship with him.

I have three children, and some things in our home are not fit for their consumption—poisonous things, yes—but they don't taste or even smell appetizing, so the chances of the kids actually eating them are rare. The enemy's so-called treats are tempting, sweet-looking, and almost as yummy as the real thing, only they leave you empty after consumption.

After noticing that my kids were on a crazy cycle of sugar mania, I decided to implement some kitchen rules. We would have plenty of fruits, vegetables, nuts, and seeds available for them to enjoy *anytime* they wanted. If they wanted to eat fruit and vegetables right before dinner, they were free to do so; I would even cut up their apples. But anything from the pantry had to be taken with permission and some things were off-limits. On family movie night, just once a week, we added their favorite treats to popcorn. Guess what? The good stuff wasn't what they craved. They had been introduced to a different kind of sweet, a different kind of fat, which controlled their tastes. We had already given them a faulty substitute too many times. It took weeks to break them of the sugar craze and back to delighting in the deliciousness of in-season strawberries.

We still have this mentality that started in the Garden of Eden: God is holding out on us; what he gives isn't as rich or satisfying as what's actually available. In the very beginning, with all the other trees available to Adam and Eve, they still ultimately chose to consume what would destroy them. We'd rather take an imitation, a manufactured goodness, than the true, organic, real goodness he keeps stocked for us. Not much has changed since our garden days. In the United States, we have nearly every conceivable resource and food source available to us. We can find watermelon in the middle of winter and oranges in the middle of summer. Even with all this abundance, we choose what we know will poison us, slowly kill us, slow us down, and inhibit our relationships because they are so deliciously tempting. God's gift of free will is the same as it's always been. He still gives us a *free* but costly choice but not before he implores us, pleads with us, and counsels us to choose life because human sin is the sorrow of God's heart. He is grieved when we choose it.

Deuteronomy 30:19 (NLT) says, "Today I have given you the choice between life and death, between blessings and curses. Now I call on heaven and earth to witness the choice you make. Oh, that you would choose life, so that you and your descendants might live!"

Generations of blessings or generations of curses: it's *your* free will choice.

Like Eve, I chose the wilderness. It started with a twinge of doubt. I thought there was more than the garden. I thought God was holding out on me, and I was hell-bent on taking whatever it was back. There I was, in the garden of the choicest fruit ever known to mankind, and I didn't trust the gardener who had given it to me.

First Timothy 6:6 tells us that godliness with contentment is great gain! I wasn't content with the godliness. My loss. Neither was Eve. We both chose the knowledge of good and evil instead of the Tree of Life. We chose to put our hope in our own knowledge, our own understanding. We unplugged from the source of power and life, and chose darkness and weakness of human flesh. The chasm without repentance, sacrificial death, and agreement became unbearably wide on purpose, so a bridge would have to be built for us to get back to him. In the desert, you have no tools to build this bridge. You can't cross it on your own, which is why so many of us try to create paradise in the wilderness, making the best of it. But God, in his great love for Adam and Eve, in his great love for you and me, saw them in their shame, their nakedness, and in his kindness and compassion, he literally made clothes for them.

"And the Lord God made clothing from animal skins for Adam and his wife" (Genesis 3:21, NLT).

When I get to heaven, this might be the first question I ask God: What did those clothes you created for Adam and Eve look like? Perfectly tailored, I'm sure. Just in case you were wondering if fashion designer is a holy enough job, it is. Yahweh was the first tailor and designer. He fashioned clothes for Adam and Eve just like he fashions clothes for us, made of mercy and love.

The kindness of God, even in our sin, is beyond my human comprehension. While Adam and Eve are blaming each other and the devil, God is creating something new, something the earth has never seen. The first sacrifice was made so that Adam and Eve would be clothed. He knew that even the first sacrifice of the animal wouldn't be a great enough exchange for their sin. He already knew a greater sacrifice would be needed. They had been moved into the wilderness, and he couldn't stand the thought of them—us—being in that place. Jesus, his Son, the ultimate, final sacrifice for sin, would need to come.

The clothes he fashioned from his kindness and love for Adam and Eve were a foreshadowing of the perfectly tailored robes of eternal righteousness he would make for all of us who believe. With the tissue and sinew from the body of Jesus Christ, he wove together garments that heal and protect now and forever. So—or should I say, "sew"—we are without shame.

"Do the riches of his extraordinary kindness make you take him for granted and despise him? Haven't you experienced how kind and understanding he has been to you? Don't mistake his tolerance for acceptance. Do you realize that all the wealth of his extravagant kindness is meant to melt your heart and lead you into repentance?" (Romans 2:4).

But at the time of our sin, Eve and I didn't even know what we couldn't see. My great Redeemer was writing an epic love story for me that would melt my heart and lead me into repentance. He was taking my sin, my destruction, and my shame and turning it into something good, something holy, even. Who does that?

The story of the fall of man reminds us that redemption's story is knit into our birth. We are part of his creation story. His plan, his purpose, and his promise is redemption for all. During adolescence, that knowledge didn't resonate in my soul the way God intended. It was twisted and distorted by the enemy as he whispered in my ear. I traded the truth for a lie without even realizing it. The understanding that I was a child born of promise and redemption became like a Tree of

> **I became the best church go-er. I was a people-pleasing, list-making, box-checking, good little Christian girl. The kind who will make any mama of a teen and twenty-something proud.**

Knowledge of Good and Evil instead of the Tree of Life. It felt like too much pressure. Along the way, that pressure turned into perfectionism. Perfectionism was built from fear of disappointing my parents, of disappointing friends and authority, of disappointing God.

I worried they wouldn't understand the temptations and struggles I faced. Instead of putting fear and pride aside to reach out, I planted myself firmly into the pew and bowed my head in pretense. I came into agreement with a spirit of religion. I became the best church go-er. I was a people-pleasing, list-making, box-checking, good little Christian girl. The kind who will make any mama of a teen and twenty-something proud. What is often bred in the church instead of passionate sons and daughters is religious zealots. And I became the best of them.

Jesus had a lot to say about and to religious zealots, it turns out. Much like the Pharisees of his day, I didn't see how I had exchanged love for the law during those years. Though seeing, I did not see; though hearing, I did not hear (Matthew 13:13, author's paraphrase). We need to know what this looks like so that we can bring grace, love, and correction that leads to freedom to those entangled by it.

Religiosity and perfectionism, with all its boundary-setting behavior, built walls around me. It separated, isolated, and made the tasks I was pursuing a higher priority than my relationship with God or others. Did I already say it isolated me? It did. Through my twenties, it kept people on the outside so that they couldn't see my vulnerability. And wouldn't you know it, staying busy made it easy for me to hide my struggles, hurts, issues, and sins too. In all that doing, I was losing my way. I had relegated God to a tiny room within the life I was constructing. My hope was in the system of the church manufactured inside the confines of comfortable appearances and Westernized ideals of success. Does this possibly look like many modern-day church go-ers in America? They are doing something, void of the Holy Spirit, in the name of progress. But come on! How could we ever accomplish anything without him?

This is how I became burnt out on church attendance, the perfectionism, the self-righteousness. When I did, I found something else to do. I tried my hand at what the world had invented. We can be sure that when we lose passion for God's way, we will see a shift within a person's life at church too. We don't just go into the world to partake; we first separate ourselves from the church, the Body of Christ, the representation of God on earth. I had already created the chasm.

A.W. Tozer explains what happens when we lose our way:

It is terrible what people will look to if they lose God. If there is no God in their eyes; and if they do not enjoy worshiping the great God Almighty that made them, they find something else to worship.

If a person does not have God, he has to have something else. Maybe it is boasts, or maybe it is money, amounting to idolatry, or going to parties or just simply raising the devil. They have lost God, and they do not know what to do, so they find something to do, which is why all the pleasures in life have been invented.[4]

From our own misunderstandings and insecurities about God's love for us, we have set the stage for a generation to be more concerned about their reputation and how they are perceived than their identity. Or to waste their identity and inheritance for the pleasures and temptations of this world.

Jesus cannot tempt us to righteous living the way the enemy can tempt us with all the pleasures of this world. We need to accept this truth and stop trying to make Jesus trendy or more appealing. The juicy Truth—Jesus—satisfies and needs no extra sauce. When you taste the real love and healing of Jesus, nothing else compares, and your cravings for everything else begin to wane. We need to trust that as we mature, the childish things will be put away. (See 1 Corinthians 13:11.) We will no longer need them.

My parents did grow out of that short-lived phase. I'm so thankful to have an earthly father and mother who continue to reflect the heavenly Father's love in an exceptional way. When you have parents like this who breathe words of faith and promise over you, it is impossible not to know Jesus. It *is* possible to forget. We forget whose we are. We become lazy about our inheritance. Our passion wanes. When we trample and defeat fear and doubt, what else could keep us from obeying, from sharing, from living in faith? Could it be our own comfort?

During the summer of 2018, I was in Haiti, serving in an orphanage where our church has ministered and fostered relationships for the last sixteen years. I love it there. It's heavenly.

On my second day there, a little girl we'll call Faye, who holds a special place in my heart, came up to me just after breakfast. I had everything in my hand preparing to leave for our day together at Vacation Bible School (VBS). She brought me a jump rope we had played with the day before that somehow, between dusk and dawn, had become all tangled up. It was tied so tightly that the plastic ends were the only straight pieces. Faye tapped me, held this jumbled mess toward me, and said with concern, "You fix?" Immediately, I placed the supplies I was carrying down onto the dusty ground, took the jump rope from her hand, and began to unravel the mess. As I did, tears began to roll down my cheeks. She waited patiently and because of my sunglasses, she couldn't see the work the Lord was doing in my heart as he was showing me, me.

See, I was untangling her mess, a mess I had no part in, and yet I was doing it with utter joy. This was why I came. I came for her. I came to help. I came to show her love in any way possible. Untangling a jump rope was building relationship and trust; it was an honor for her to reach out to me, and I didn't take it lightly.

In that moment, the Lord reminded me of all my tangled jump ropes. He showed me how easily he could untangle my mess, and most importantly, he blew my mind when I realized it was his joy to do so. He wasn't mad at me. That, after all, was why Jesus came. As the tears streamed down my face, Faye waited patiently for me to do something she knew she couldn't do, something she knew I *could* do. The Lord spoke again.

"You honor me when you come to me. You don't have to do anything but rest in me, knowing that I complete the work. Would you give Faye a half-tangled jump rope back? Neither would I give you a mess that's only half-way worked out. I'm faithful to complete it. I put it all in order."

Somehow, in the midst of the poorest nation in the Western Hemisphere, I knew it was true. Vast amounts of work still need to be done in Haiti. I was untangling one jump rope for one fatherless child, yet hope endured in me. He is setting it right because Jesus's work in us is never almost. It's all. It's complete.

This sinful life, this life that offers death, starts out with just a few wrong agreements here or there. It's like tying small knots into the rope of your life. It's just a few exchanges of the knowledge of God for the knowledge of good and evil. Until finally, you've forgotten about freedom. I welcomed the perhaps scenarios instead of engaging in the promises. My life became about me and what seemed to be the best option. *Perhaps this is it,* I often wondered.

That night, when I met that guy at the bar, that's what I thought. *Perhaps.*

When he asked me to marry him, that's what I thought. *Perhaps.*

When I agreed to his proposal, that's what I thought. *Perhaps.*

When I walked down the aisle with my doubts, that's what I thought. *Perhaps.*

After I got married, I became unbelievably depressed. I gained fifty pounds and cried obsessively over the direction of my life. I felt as if I had betrayed myself. I hated my job, my apartment, and the life I had willingly said yes to, the life I thought I so desperately wanted. I was so eager to find temporary relief from where I was living that when temptation presented itself, I didn't have to deliberate for very long. I opened the door to all kinds of behaviors that temporarily buried my shame and my pain.

I unleashed a torrent of more *perhaps* exchanges. When I was driving home drunk after partying all night, that's what I thought. When I was in the bed of a man who wasn't my husband, that's what I thought, *Perhaps this is it.* And with every heartbreaking, outside-of-God's-will-and-promise decision

I made, I locked myself into a prison, fastening more and more chains to create an impossible mess. In my prison cell, I had forgotten about freedom. I looked down, and my life had become all knotted up until I could see nothing but plastic handles.

I couldn't understand the decisions that I was making even though I knew they were wrong. This created an unmatched and unbearable anxiety within me. I was starting to crumble. Depression, fueled by anger toward myself, knocked on my door incessantly. I participated. I escaped. I made many regrettable choices during my twenties, namely, cheating on my husband. That moniker was the whopper, the identity thief. With that decision, my address changed. I built a home in that cell. I couldn't escape or separate who I was to God from what my sin meant to me. The chasm was too wide. It seemed so much easier for me to find my identity in that shame instead of repentance.

Romans 1:21–23 tells us, "Throughout human history the fingerprints of God were upon them, yet they refused to honor him as God or even be thankful for his kindness. Instead, they entertained corrupt and foolish thoughts about what God was like. This left them with nothing but misguided hearts, steeped in moral darkness. Although claiming to be super-intelligent, they were in fact shallow fools. For only a fool would trade the unfading splendor of the immortal God to worship the fading image of other humans, idols made to look like people, animals, birds, and even creeping reptiles!"

I bowed my head in shame and agreement. And the more I did it, the more I justified my actions, and the less shame I felt. I worshipped at the altar of indifference and numbed my aching soul with all the pleasures available to me. I quieted the voice of God, which is a certain recipe for the death of faith and hope. This deadly recipe baked up quite a concoction. Until finally, I had spent more months in unfaithfulness than in faithfulness. I had made a mockery of our covenant. I had sinned against God, my husband, the men I had slept with, and myself. I was in bondage to the father of lies instead of being the freedom fighter for the Spirit of Truth that he calls me to be. God still knew who I was, but I no longer recognized myself.

I was the joker, the fool, the adulteress.

## LET'S REFLECT:

What areas of your own faith do you question?

What temptations are you facing?

Is there someone who *seems* to have it all together but is beginning to pull away from family, church life, or honoring friendships?

How can you regularly reach out to that person to bring truth and love?

What practical steps can you take to combat and overcome temptation? For some guidance, see Matthew 4:1–11 when Satan tempted Jesus in the wilderness.

YOU'VE GIVEN ME A MILLION CHANCES

TO TURN AND LOOK YOUR WAY

BUT I WANT SO BADLY TO CONTROL

I BACKED MYSELF INTO THIS CAVE

I FEEL SO TIRED.

**"I CAN'T ESCAPE"**

**VALLEY'S END**

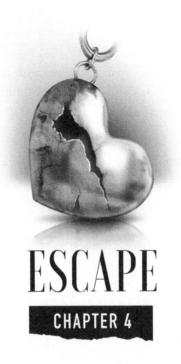

# ESCAPE

## CHAPTER 4

I have never spent the night in jail. Praise the Lord! He has had his hand on me, for there were plenty of times my behavior would have warranted a night or two in lock up. I worked at a family-style pub through my junior and senior year in college. We closed early enough so we could catch the late-night campus parties most nights. If we couldn't find a party, we could head over to the bar on campus.

One night, some friends and I arrived too late for us to have the wonderful night we were hoping for, so after the bar closed, we hung out in between the campus convenience store and the bar. This spot was a small park with soft grass. A full moon was shining, and we were enjoying the spring Florida early morning hours at our perfect location. But we had two problems: no one had any beer, and no one wanted to leave to buy any. What should we do? Ever the problem-solving leader, I noticed that the convenience store was still open. We could grab another round there and continue our late-night picnic as planned. We all pitched in some money, and I ran over to grab the drinks we needed to keep the party alive. But there was a slight issue; it was after one a.m., the deadline for all alcohol sales. While the store was still open, the beer cases were padlocked with makeshift wiring that stretched like a big X across the three glass cases. I decided to just ignore that and slip my arm into the locked glass case and slide out two, six-packs of beer.

While I was scoping out the scene, I made friends with the attending clerk, who I assumed was a year or two older than me. I slapped the twenty dollars on the glass counter and told him to look away with a determined smile. I grabbed the case of Miller Light from behind the locked doors and slipped outside. I whispered to myself, "Well, looks like I'll never be mayor," as I looked up at the camera that hung over the exit. But the police never came to get me. The clerk never said a single word. He probably used that twenty dollars to buy his own beer that night. My friends cheered and laughed at my so-called courage. I was the star of the night. We stayed up way too late, partying into the wee hours of the morning.

Goodness, I wish that story was about someone else. Maybe I've never spent one night in a physical jail. But because of stories like these, I spent many years imprisoned by my sin. I had done so many wrong things for so many years that I couldn't escape what my sin told me about myself. I wanted to believe that if I could just change _____, then maybe I wouldn't hate myself so much. So, I tried reinventing myself a few times.

Eventually, my initial bout of infidelity was exposed to my husband, but after some difficult conversations, we decided to stay together—not out of forgiveness but out of duty. Neither one of us forgave me. My guilt and shame successfully kept this particular sin at bay for a year or two. I reinvented us. We became more involved at church and did our best to keep working through our differences. I lost the fifty pounds I had gained; we bought a house, and I found a job in real estate that I loved.

Check. Check. Check.

Still, no matter where I went or how much I reinvented myself, I remained a prisoner. A prisoner of my own sin. The circumstances never needed to change. The soul—the seat of your mind, will, and emotions—must be transformed, as Romans 12:1–2 tells us. Sin locks you into a new but false identity. I'm not the only one who has found themselves chained up by sin a time or two.

Here's what Paul says about it in Romans 7:22–23: "Truly, deep within my true identity, I love to do what pleases God. But I discern another power operating in my humanity, waging a war against the moral principles of my conscience and bringing me into captivity as a prisoner to the "law" of sin—this unwelcome intruder in my humanity."

What are we to do with this truth? What is the remedy? What is the hope that Paul clings to after he reveals his struggle? Jesus. Jesus renews his mind. Jesus tells him who he really is. Just as it was for Paul, Jesus became my escape into redemption, and my redemption was imminent.

In the third year of our marriage, we were asked to lead our church's building campaign. We hurriedly stepped up to leadership and service together. I thought service in the church would save me from myself. But friends, I can promise you this: The busyness of church programs doesn't save you. It never will. During this time and unbeknownst to anyone else, my husband was sleeping in the room down the hall. We were a hot mess, bound up by our many issues. We didn't reveal a single one of them to anyone, keeping up appearances like any good Christian couple should.

Oh, perfectionism. You're still here? Great.

One night, during this time, I woke up from the strangest dream. I had gone on a date with my sales partner. After the date, he kissed me, and I didn't cringe. This was odd because, while I was friendly with my partner, he wasn't my type, I knew he was seriously involved with his girlfriend. And I was doing my best to keep my act together now, ya know, since I was *married*. In addition to this—and almost as important to me as my marriage vows—was the fact that I didn't want to complicate or ruin my future career. Bleh.

The day after my dream, I went to work and suddenly couldn't look at this guy in the same way. Something awoke in me. I acted in haste, worried that I would destroy my job by harboring the feelings that came from this dream. Instead of taking those thoughts captive and making them obedient to Christ, I reasoned that the best way to deal with this would be to tell him so that we could laugh it off. I told him at lunch the next day. Bless my heart.

**Like an iron ball, shame kept me rooted to that spot so that I couldn't move forward into who God destined me to be.**

Oh, the drama I used to live in. You guys, I nearly drowned in the drama I created.

Dear Jesus, thank you for not laughing at me or chiding me when I made all those stupid decisions. How lovely and patient you are. I can't believe I didn't drive you crazy or away.

As soon as I spilled the details of my dream, I figured he would join me in a jolly laugh; we would pay the check, and be on our way back to work. But his expression said something different. His eyes said, "Yes," as though I had just given him an invitation. Looking back, I'm sure it was. Just five days later, we were physically involved.

While involved in this new affair and also on a mission trip to the Bayou to serve those affected by Hurricane Katrina—because apparently I couldn't escape my calling, no matter the sin I was in—I had some time to reflect on what my life had become.

**I penned this in my journal:**

*I'm sorry, Lord. I do love you. Why do I sin and do what I know I shouldn't do? God, you are so awesome and eager to forgive me . . . why? I am such a sinner. So unworthy to help people, to be used by you. Let me hear you. Help me to stay focused on you and the plan you have for me. Even now, as I pray and reflect, my thoughts turn to a place they shouldn't. Why do I sin? Why do I keep sinning? Why am I not making the right decisions when temptation comes? I am bearing no fruit right now. Lord, I need your help. I am not worthy. Every day, I feel like a failure.*

I couldn't figure out how I had become a lying, cheating, depressed, lost person again. Sin was the chain holding me in my cell, but what made it difficult to move wasn't the sin but what was tethered to the sin: shame. Like an iron ball, shame kept me rooted to that spot so that I couldn't move forward into who God destined me to be. Since I couldn't go anywhere else, sin did just what Jesus warned it would do in John 8:34. It continued to wrap chains around me like I was a slave. I was bound by it, bound to it, bound to do it. It became my god, consuming my thoughts. I surrendered my will to it more times than I can count. Because of my separation from God, I no longer knew who I was in Christ, so I identified myself by my sin and shame. That was the enemy's doing. That is how he operates. He identifies you by your sins and fears and failures. He tells you that you are condemned. But God always calls you by your name, by your relationship with him—my daughter, my son, my child—with *love* and *hope*. Shame, I thought, knew my name: adulteress. But Jesus said, "Erin, because of my blood, you're unadulterated. You've been purified. You're undefiled. Agree with who I've made you to be." It would be many years before I could let forgiveness do that good work in me.

This lying and cheating continued until I was in the fourth year of marriage. I had become a professional at living a double life. All that juggling was really exhausting, though. My day job was the only safe place free from drama or disgrace. The afterhours were scandalous. I went from secret meetings to church meetings, sometimes within hours. I don't even recognize the girl I used to be. Nonetheless, that was me. And you can't know the power of resurrection unless you know the life and death that came before it. In all this, my heart is not to focus on sin but for grace to be grasped and glorified. With that reminder, let's keep going.

That's more a prompt for me than you, I imagine.

The guy from work and I were becoming serious. Hearts were involved now. It was more than I had bargained for. I hadn't wanted to fall in love with anybody. I didn't want to be the first one in my marriage to leave. But sin snowballs. My husband and I were further apart than ever. I couldn't hate myself anymore, so I began to despise him. We separated ourselves from our leadership and service roles at church, and instead, I spent hours analyzing the details of my escape from a marriage I no longer felt was right for me. I saw a desert landscape around me, a barren land, and I thought my marriage and my husband were causing it, not my own unfaithfulness, not my separation from God. In my haste to relieve my heart and head from leading a double life, I tried to build a bridge of escape from the barren land of the desert. I devised what I thought was a full-proof plan to eliminate one of the lives I was living.

Never has there been a more elaborate and perfectly conspired plan than this one schemed up at the height of my stress and doubt. The best plans are hatched this way. I'm sure that's what all the Proverbs point to. Ha! No.

Proverbs 6:12–13 tells us, "Here's another life lesson to learn from observing the wayward and wicked man. You can tell

they are lawless. They're constant *liars*, proud deceivers, full of clever ploys and convincing plots" (emphasis added).

My plan went like this:

- ❑ Separate from husband for reasons of "irreconcilable differences"
- ❑ Lay low
- ❑ Divorce husband
- ❑ Keep affair quiet
- ❑ Wait for an appropriate amount of time
- ❑ Introduce new boyfriend (current boyfriend) to family
- ❑ Wait for an appropriate amount of time
- ❑ Get married
- ❑ Have perfect wedding
- ❑ Tell no one, ever.

What a fool I had become.

❧

Proverbs 26:12 says, "There's only one thing worse than a fool, and that's the smug, conceited man always in love with his own opinions."

I had become both, for I was in love with this foolish plan.

My husband and I went through the motions of counseling. I had promised I would go, and in some deep place in my heart, I might have even hoped it would work. But it didn't because it would've required me to be honest. I wasn't willing to do that as I hadn't practiced honesty in a very long time. Instead, my head and heart had moved on to task one: leave current husband. A few months before our fourth wedding anniversary, I did just that. I left and moved in with my newlywed sister.

My plan was still intact. I simply had to lay low for a few months until the motions for divorce were finalized. I was celebrating my great escape late in the moonlight, out with my boyfriend, when a family member happened to see me and my new boyfriend, Mickey, getting a little too close for comfort.

Suddenly, in the mirage that was an oasis of my desert, I was exposed and so ashamed. And like my friend, Eve, I suddenly realized I was naked in the garden. It was all so confusing. The fruit I had eaten looked delicious, but it was poisonous and deadly. Too late, I could see it for what it was. The damage was done. This was not the way back to God, so when God asked me where I was, I couldn't hear him.

In John 8:43–45, Jesus says to the Pharisees, who seemed like they, more than anyone, would know and recognize the voice of God:

> "Why don't you understand what I say? You don't understand because your hearts are closed to my message! You are the offspring of your father, the devil, and you serve your father very well, passionately carrying out his desires. He's been a murderer right from the start! He never stood with the One who is the true Prince, for he's full of nothing but lies—lying is his native tongue. He is a master of deception and the father of lies! But I am the true Prince who speaks nothing but the truth, yet you refuse to believe and you want nothing to do with me."

You guys, I was so good at compartmentalizing my sin. The interruption of my family member into this sizzling rendezvous was *shock-ing*. I was not living out one bit of truth in my life, unless you count the pleasure I pursued. That was my only honest pursuit. I was passionately carrying out the desires of a murderer. I had killed my marriage. There was no going back.

I ignored that still, small voice one last time when I signed the divorce papers just a month after our fourth wedding anniversary.

And instead of depending on grace conceived in repentance, I stayed the course of slavery. I had picked up that burden of shame and carried it around as if it were my kid. I guess it was, so like a slave, I believed this was my lot in life, my burden to bear, my screaming toddler. I had just stayed in those chains for so long that I started thinking and acting like a slave, like someone with no rights, no power. I believed lies that said:

- ❏ You're a cheater.
- ❏ You'll never be trusted again.
- ❏ You'll lose your reputation.
- ❏ Your parents will be crushed.
- ❏ Your family will lose all respect for you.
- ❏ You'll never be forgiven.
- ❏ You won't have any friends.
- ❏ You're a liar.
- ❏ You'll be asked to leave the church.
- ❏ You will be left with nothing.
- ❏ You *are* nothing.

All the while, Jesus was beckoning me, "Are you weary, carrying a heavy burden? Then come to me. I will refresh your life, for I am your oasis Simply join your life with mine. Learn my ways and you'll discover that I'm gentle, humble, easy to please. You will find refreshment and rest in me. For all that I require of you will be pleasant and easy to bear" (Matthew 11:28–30).

I didn't hear him. I didn't tell him. I didn't tell anybody.

I quickly made an excuse for that stolen kiss to my family member, claiming temporary relief from the trauma of a broken marriage. I was still hiding and covering up so much. I perpetuated a lie that *nothing* had been going on before my ex-husband and I had separated. Nobody knew the extent of my mistakes or the depth of my debauchery. Since the divorce was final, I figured Mickey and I could now officially date without attracting too many raised eyebrows. And I was ready for that. I was ready to introduce him to my family. I was ready to leave my old life far behind me so that my new life could start. I was ready to move on from my divorce as if nothing had happened, as if I hadn't broken vows or destroyed a covenant with God, as if I hadn't hurt people or severed relationships. All I cared about was keeping my reputation intact.

We often consider our sins in the light of morality versus immorality, but the sin we find ourselves in is not simply the engagement. I didn't see then that my sin occurred long before I committed adultery with my body. My heart was far from the Lord. The actions simply followed where my heart led. Our sin is found in who or what has our hearts and the decisions we make because our hearts belong to something or someone besides Jesus. My own desires sat on the throne of my heart. So all I did was serve myself.

## LET'S REFLECT:

Think about a moment when you looked at yourself in the mirror and suddenly didn't recognize the person you had become. Did the change happen overnight or was it gradual? When did the change start?

Have you ever confessed those sins to the Lord? Have you ever allowed his forgiveness to empower you to forgive yourself?

Have you forgiven others and even yourself, but you still feel held back by the weight of the ball and chain of shame? Pause here. Take a few minutes to hear what he has to say about you. Write his words of love down. Speak them over yourself and allow his words to let you move forward into all he has for you.

WHEN ALL AROUND ME IS FALLING

IN THE MADNESS YOU ARE CALLING

I CAN HEAR, I CAN HEAR YOU NOW.  .

**"I CAN HEAR YOU NOW"**

**VALLEY'S END**

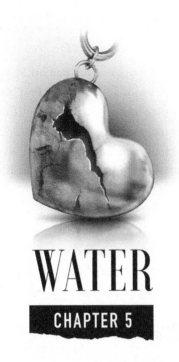

# WATER

**CHAPTER 5**

It turns out my carefully laid plans were about to crumble, exposing my scandalous living in the most dramatic way possible for my family—and everyone—to see.

While I was "waiting for an appropriate amount of time," I found out I was pregnant.

Like that tangled jump rope, I now had a jumbled mess of knots to unravel.

Sometimes right before we're headed out the door, I'll grab a necklace from my closet. When I pull it off my dresser, I find that several are attached to it and tangled up together. That's what my life looked like in those weeks. I had dragged some people into this mess with me, and I had to figure out a way to make it right. I had to do it while I was in a hurry, all at once, all by myself. Have you ever been there?

I wanted to run and hide and conceal and do anything to continue to cover it up. I couldn't bear the thought of my parents knowing for certain that their good, Christian girl wasn't innocent and holy and pure like they had assumed. My recent divorce had already tainted my formerly perfect image. I didn't want to further mar their impression of me and confirm their worst fears. I was too afraid. I felt trapped by all those lies, all that hiding, all those secrets. I couldn't package this any other way.

My reputation was the cornerstone of my life. Everything else was built on that shoddy workmanship. If it crumbled, so did my identity. All my worst fears were realized—my sin, my nakedness, fully exposed—my parents seeing the raw and unfiltered image of me, their trust betrayed. I was sick. There now seemed to be no escape. I was at the end of my tangled rope.

> **I couldn't bear the thought of my parents knowing for certain that their good, Christian girl wasn't innocent and holy and pure like they had assumed.**

The minutes and hours that made up those days were gut-wrenching and the very worst of my life. I have never felt as defeated, humiliated, and ashamed as I did then. I contemplated every possible option—no matter how extreme. Abortion? Yes. Job transfer? In a heartbeat. Suicide? It was a fleeting thought. Cut off communication with family? Sadly, yeah.

Those dead ends have a purpose. This became the place where every other alternative carried steep consequences that led to the real death of human beings, relationships, and trust. And once I faced those consequences and realized the severity of my situation, I knew there was only one way out.

Remember our dear friends of the faith, Abraham and Sarah? I've got some wonderful news! Her story didn't end with her word, perhaps. Hagar, her maidservant, did conceive a son, Ishmael. Jealousy and envy ravaged Sarah's relationship with Hagar and Abraham, and like me, I'm sure she became a less hopeful version of herself. I imagine she believed she had missed the promise completely, feeling as if she was moved out of God's hand of grace and covenant and was destined to watch other people walk in blessing. She and Abraham were past the ages of fertility. Hope was not only diminished, it was lost. Done. The natural laws of this world had stolen their hope along with the season of conception from them. What more did she have to look forward to? She felt as if life were hopeless without children of her own. I imagine she was waiting to die. A promise from God twisted and forfeited due to our own sin feels like death. I felt dead in my sin too. I suppose we must be the most surrendered in life when we are contemplating death.

Then one day, hope came down for a visit. The Lord in three persons dropped by to chat with Abraham and Sarah. Isn't that crazy? As she listened in on the conversation that *God* was having with her husband, she heard her name. These words were spoken over her, "I will return to you about this time next year, and your wife, Sarah, will have a son!" (Genesis 18:10, NLT).

To which she fell face down, praising God.

Oh, wait a minute. Nope. That's not how it happened. She laughed. She laughed because Sarah was as human and fallible as any of us. At that moment, heaven came down to fill her with hope, but she couldn't conceive it or receive it. Instead her laugh mocked the hope of a miracle. It was a laugh of, "I'll believe it when I see it." It was condescending and bitter from the overflow of her aching heart. The Lord asked her why she laughed, and instead of leaning in toward honesty and the brokenness of her soul, she lied. But why?

Like Sarah, I couldn't conceive of his love. It was laughable that God could or would want to do anything with me. I had made a mockery of his promises, twisted them and exchanged them for selfish ambition. I had laughed in the face of his goodness and love toward me.

In our most vulnerable moments, we can make wrong agreements about the nature of God. We can forget who he is, but God cannot go against his own promises. He says to us in his relentless pursuit of our hearts, "My covenant is my covenant; my blessing is my blessing; my promise is my promise; my Word is my Word, regardless of your sin. I stand true to it." (See Psalm 89:34.)

As physically sick as the thought made me, the only way to untie the knots, to build the bridge to freedom, was to tell the truth. I knew I didn't have the strength to do it on my own, so I reverted to the only thing I thought could save me: I prayed the most honest and panicked of prayers.

They were unlike any prayers I had ever prayed before. They weren't pious and lukewarm. They were tearful laments. They were far from hopeful but filled with longing. They were desperate pleas to a merciful God. I wasn't sure that I wanted him to answer me. I wasn't sure that he was very happy to hear from me. I wasn't sure if he would be loving or vengeful. I just wanted to know that he was still there, like my kids do when I am outside the stall at a public restroom. They call for me because they want to know that I haven't left them there in that nasty place, all alone. I was calling for him because I was certain no one else would stay there with me, in that prison, in those chains. But I was hoping he would.

Somehow, when I was praying panicked prayers to God, withholding full disclosure of my brokenness, I felt his hand of promise on me and his words of love and blessing over me. I didn't know how the situation would work out but somewhere in that place, I knew he hadn't forgotten about me. That was enough for me in that moment.

What other god comes down in the midst of our anguish to remind us of his presence and promise? Only him.

The Samaritan woman in John 4 got this kind of reminder in the midst of her pain. She was wrestling with her own understanding of the God of restoration. In those days, women typically drew water in the mornings or evenings because it was a much cooler time of day. On this trek for water, the women of the village would congregate and talk. Similar to the conversations we women have as we gather for coffee these days, these women gathered around the town's well back then. But you wouldn't have found the Samaritan woman among them. She was considered scandalous due to her involvement with many men over the years. She longed to escape moral prejudice from the life of sin she had chosen. She, like me, wanted to escape the judgments of her community and even her own shame, so she went to draw water in the afternoon, in the heat of the day, instead of in the morning, to avoid running into any other women. She nears the source of water, and here she finds Jesus sitting on Jacob's Well. That well and its namesake, Jacob, had a history. And Jesus knew all about it, which is precisely why he sat himself there.

The Samaritan woman and I could relate to the character of Jacob. He, like us, had spent years ashamed and in hiding. He was on the run from his brother, whose inheritance and blessing he had stolen by deceiving his own father. Jacob also spent years working for his soon-to-be father-in-law in order to earn the right to marry his beloved. As if that weren't enough striving for one man, he also spent an entire night wrestling with God. This all came just before God renamed him Israel, blessed him, and restored his relationship with his long-lost brother, Esau.

The Samaritan woman and I would learn, like Jacob, that God appoints our times of wrestling with him. He says, "You've been running too long. It's time to stop your striving."

This is exactly what Jesus intends to do when he is found sitting on top of this well, interrupting the daily task performed by this child of God, the Samaritan woman. The commentary in *the Passion Translation Bible* gives us insight into the significance of the throne Jesus chose to perch himself upon that day.

"The well was "a spring-fed well." This becomes a picture of the "spring" of the Jacob-life inside of every one of us. Fed by Adam's fall, this spring has flowed through all humanity. But Jesus sat as a "lid" to Jacob's well, sealing its polluted stream. In Christ, Jacob's clever striving has ended. A living well became a lid to Jacob's well as Jesus sat there ready to give his living water to all who would come and drink. A well sitting upon a well."[5]

Here, Jesus is inviting her to wrestle with him. And it's necessary because she is tired of walking through the desert in the heat of the day, tired of hiding in shame. She is weary. She is thirsty. As was I. I didn't know how much I needed a break from my clever striving, slaving to keep my two lives perfectly separated. Jesus was inviting me in those weeks to contend with him.

As if to say, "C'mon, Erin. Bring it. Whatever it is, I can handle it. I will wrestle those things from your death grip if I have to. I know you're tired of holding onto them. So let's go. I'm not giving up on you." Those words of truth felt like a cup of water being drawn up from a well—just a bit of water in the middle of my desert wilderness. I was looking for some quick relief in this cup, some penance, some prayer that would resurrect me. It was enough of an invitation for me to relent in my unbelief and have the first of many honest conversations with the Lord. It sounded a lot like the conversation Jesus had with the Samaritan woman. Let's dive deeper into her story.

"Soon a Samaritan woman came to draw water. Jesus said to her, 'Give me a drink of water'" (John 4:6–8).

*Soon a pregnant woman came looking for relief. Jesus said to her, "Give me your heart."*

"Surprised, she said, 'Why would a Jewish man ask a Samaritan woman for a drink of water?'" (John 4:9).

*Surprised, I said, "Why would the Son of God ask such a sinful woman for her heart?"*

"Jesus replied, 'If you only knew who I am and the gift that God wants to give you—you'd ask me for a drink, and I would give to you living water'" (John 4:10).

*Jesus replied, "If you only knew the kind of giver I am and the gift that is available to you outside of this desert. You'd ask me for relief, and I would blow your mind with my plans to heal your burdened heart."*

"The woman replied, 'But sir, you don't even have a bucket and this well is very deep. So where do you find this "living water"? Do you really think that you are greater than our ancestor Jacob who dug this well and drank from it himself, along with his children and livestock?'" (John 4:11–12).

*I replied, "How could you possibly do this in me when I am such a mess? You don't know the half of what I've done. I doubt you could get me, Mickey, and this new baby out of this hot mess. No chance."*

"Jesus answered, 'If you drink from Jacob's well you'll be thirsty again and again, but if anyone drinks the living water I give them, they will never thirst again and will be forever satisfied! For when you drink the water I give you it becomes a gushing fountain of the Holy Spirit, springing up and flooding you with endless life!'" (John 4:13–14).

*Jesus answered, "If you try to free yourself, you will fail, but if you come to me, I will free you, and you'll be free forever. You'll stand firm on a foundation of faith. I will give you an abundant, ever-lasting life, a life you could never imagine."*

I couldn't conceive of this, but it was and remains my best option to trust him. I didn't understand the doubt that I was surrendering at the time.

I certainly didn't realize that I had exchanged it for hope, but the evidence of peace that came from those panicked prayers motivated Mickey and me to move forward. We agreed that we would meet with my parents, finally come out of hiding, and stop ignoring the voice that had been asking me, as I wandered in the desert, like Adam and Eve in the garden, "Where are you?"

He doesn't ask us these questions because he doesn't know the answer; he asks us because we need to realize that *we* don't know.

That day, I was beginning to understand that I didn't know where I was or how I had gotten there. I was lost. If I didn't know where I was or how I got there, then logic would reason that I didn't know how to find my way out. How appropriate that Jesus is called The Way. He helps us find our way out when we're lost.

Oh, the enduring patience of God. I look back and imagine him relieved and rejoicing, "Finally! Can we get out of here already?"

## LET'S REFLECT:

Stop here and take the time to dive into the well of God's grace. God withholds his judgment from those who love him, because of Jesus.

What's keeping you from seeking forgiveness and finding love, mercy, and grace? Is it unbelief (fear) or unworthiness (pride)?

When have you twisted and forfeited one of God's promises because of your own sin?

Are you in a desperate place like I was? Ashamed? Defeated? Contemplating death? Emmanuel, God with us, is with you, right now, right where you are.

Will you let him lead you out of your mess? Will you take the drink of living water that he offers so freely?

I CAN'T ESCAPE

YOUR LOVE FOR ME

CAUGHT UP HERE IN YOUR WONDER

I COME UNDONE IN YOUR LOVE

NO, I CAN'T ESCAPE.

**"I CAN'T ESCAPE"**

**VALLEY'S END**

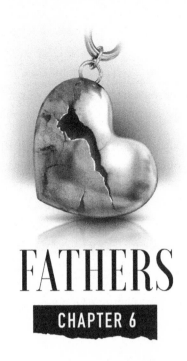

# FATHERS

## CHAPTER 6

My dad, an incredible musician, used to soothe his restless children to sleep singing songs of love and truth with his guitar. Sometimes the words came from his own heart; other times, he sang old or new church hymns; other times, it was Tina Turner, the Beatles, Neil Young, or James Taylor. My favorites were the calming strums of his acoustic guitar played in the moonlight by my bed. It looked so much like heaven to me. Before I could wrap my feeble mind around the thought of heaven, I felt it there. There was safety, my earthly father, and my heavenly One, singing me into my dreams.

I come from a long line of musicians, teachers of music, vocalists, worshipers, and song writers. Even as I write this, my little sister is in a recording studio just a few feet away. She and her band are recording a song she wrote inspired by my story of grace and surrender. I can't even stay in there to listen. I cry a puddle of tears every time I walk in. She is walking in her purpose. She is living a calling that is part of her very DNA. It fits her beautifully.

Your identity in Christ is just everything. Let's talk about it forever. The talents, gifts, and purpose he has knit into us is a legacy we pass on to our children.

By seeing my parents use their gifts and talents for the Lord, they sewed into my fiber from a young age a deep sense of purpose that I couldn't fully comprehend growing up. It was coupled with the idea that surrender is the only place to live, that it takes time, that it's a process, but we serve a Father who won't give up on us. Our hope should remain in him because he's called us his very own children. He, above anyone, is a Father to be trusted.

> "And because we are his children, God has sent the Spirit of his Son into our hearts, prompting us to call out, 'Abba, Father'" (Galatians 4:6, NLT).

While a legacy of blessing passes from one generation to another, curses can also pass from one generation to another. Remember, he always places both options before us. Physically you inherit traits that belonged to your parents and grandparents. Emotionally you likely received qualities and temperaments that run in the family as well. What occurs in the physical world is merely a shadow of what occurs in the spiritual realm. Unless and until we identify these and defeat them by agreeing with the Word of God, we are subjected to them. We are slaves to the curse of the law until we overcome the law through God's love shown by the sacrificial death of Jesus Christ. The curse of the law leads to death, which is broken by the breath of Christ upon each curse to deliver us into resurrection living and blessing so that we aren't bound to it. I'll say that again: your spiritual legacy can change as you receive the inheritance your heavenly Father has given you. We must acknowledge and repent for the sins of our fathers lest we repeat the sin ourselves and leave it as an unwanted inheritance to our children.

Think about it for a moment. Is there a theme in your family lineage? Search the past and present. Through out the generations of your family, can you identify patterns of prejudice, alcoholics, workaholics, sex-addicts, drug-addicts, fatherless, motherless, homeless or consistently living in some other dire place. You can't change the choices your family made in the past. But now, you can identify those broken places and let the freedom of Jesus remove that curse over you. With him, you can choose life.

My parents first met in high school. She was from a military family and moved to Findlay, Ohio, her senior year. When she, a new student, walked into my dad's classroom, my dad ran home and told his mom he had met the woman he would marry. But she would only have him as a friend. His overwhelming patience served him well many times in their marriage, just as it did while he was in the friend zone. Their friendship blossomed as they went off to college. She, an art major an hour away from him, and he, a gifted musician, saw each other on weekends during their first semesters of college. They had so much to talk about then—the war, the draft, music, drugs, the movements, the resistance, the politics. Those were the conversations through which their love grew. The friendship gave way to intense passion, and one summer night, she became pregnant.

She was devastated by the news, as she knew her parents would be upset. Courageously, this new young couple with the whole mad world in front of them went hand in hand to her father's home—folks called him the Colonel—shortly after the discovery. This up-and-coming musician confessed his sin, asking for permission and blessing to marry the woman of his dreams, but the Colonel denied his request. Looking directly at his daughter that evening, he simply said, "It takes two to tango." That was that. The disappointment in his eyes was as clear as his words. His wife, Butch, as he called her, for her ability to speak truth to him when no one else dared, stood alongside him without a word.

My mother and father walked in shame out the door and to the guitarist's home, where his family sat, praying for their three sons. One was serving his second tour in Vietnam; one was serving as a reservist in the National

Guard, and one, their youngest, still seemed aimless. In they walked, hand in hand, shocked, desperate, scared, and ashamed. But there, in a small kitchen, in a modest home, just off Main Street, they found love. They found acceptance. They found help. They scraped together some money from the modest means of the guitarist's family. With it, they were able to buy the Colonel's daughter a bouquet, alter a second-hand yellow dress, and reserve a tiny space at the Holiday Inn outside of town to host a celebration for one side of the family. The other side wouldn't show.

**I grew up with a certainty that I was the by-product of God's redemptive plan. I was a collateral blessing.**

The honeymoon wouldn't end for the guitarist. For my mom, the late-night gigs, watching friends lose themselves to drugs, and experiencing the highs and lows of pregnancy were as hard as an Ohio winter. Butch knew the depths of her daughter's pain, so she secretly sent her youngest daughter money so that the newlyweds could make a life away from the noise of a small town. They made their way to Florida just before the arrival of their first-born son. The year was 1971.

Many odd jobs and seven years later, the Colonel's daughter had grown tired of Suitcase City (another name for a section of Tampa), transient friends, the guitarist's pursuit of fame, and the demands of two kids. Butch had slowly built a bridge so that she could see her grandchildren. By now, the Colonel was coming around too. His daughter had grown weary from fighting for a husband that was long on love but short on provision. She said the words that would send her young husband into a frenzied search for salvation: "I want a divorce."

Filled with fear, the guitarist immediately flew home to the rural Ohio town where they had met. Upon his arrival, his dad invited him to a men's retreat at his parish. Desperate and hopeless, he went along. Truth filled his longing heart as his father spoke these words of life to him. "Whenever I am in a desperate place, I find my way to Jesus."

That weekend, the guitarist did too. He found himself at the feet of Jesus, the cross, fully surrendered. My dad raced back to Florida with all his newfound truth and told his bride what had happened in a last-ditch attempt to save their marriage. The alternative? He would find himself standing before her with no choice but to sign the papers, finalizing their divorce. But in God's divine plan, in the late evening of a hot summer night in Florida, my dad led my mom to the saving grace of Jesus Christ. Less than a year later, I was born.

After this moment of surrender, everything changed. My dad found a stable job and reserved his amazing talent as a musician for the church. With the guidance of the Lord, my mom mended the relationship with her parents that had been strained for so many years. As kids, while gathered around the family table, eating bologna sandwiches, we heard many stories of these two people known by so many as "the Colonel" and "Butch." We just called them MeMaw and Poppee.

I grew up with a certainty that I was the by-product of God's redemptive plan. I was a collateral blessing. If the enemy would've had his way, my parents would've divorced, and I would've never been born. *But God.* He did have a plan. He does have a purpose. Hope revealed itself to my parents, and they were never the same.

My parents struggled a lot in those early years, because of their own mistakes. They didn't know the consequences of their sin. They didn't think about how their choices affected people they loved. Sometimes people see life through a cloudy lens of their perceptions, their guilt, their heartache, and their trauma. When we think they'll react in love or acceptance, they suddenly shift. They go left when we think they will go right. They disappoint us because we expect something from them. Expectation kills relationships, but hope restores them. Expectation steals; hope reveals.

This story played in my mind on the way to their house that January night. They didn't know this side of me. They weren't ready to hear this story Mickey and I were bound to tell. This would be confusing and hurtful. I knew it. I had condemned myself before we even arrived. Whatever their disappointment and reaction, I knew I deserved it. I expected many different reactions from them. I was ready for long explanations, for accusations, for scary questions, for hurt feelings, and for angry words. I was prepared for tears of disappointment and broken hearts and for them to need time to process. I braced myself for the same type of rejection they had experienced.

We stepped into an empty nest. All the kids were grown, and my parents now lived in a little maintenance-free villa, different from where I was raised. But familiar items remained the same. Pictures of their four children and five grandchildren were everywhere; the art that flanked the walls of my childhood home was there, too, and my dad's guitar leaned against the wall in the corner of the den. But the most recognizable welcome came as my parents wrapped their loving arms around us, inviting us into their home. They were polite with Mickey although they had only met him once. These were less than ideal circumstances, but I couldn't change them. I was too exhausted to try it my way anymore.

We didn't spend too much time on niceties. Mickey and I sat hand in hand on the broad cream couch, my dad in his La-Z-Boy to our right, my mom in her upholstered rocker to the left. The moment of truth had arrived. Mickey looked my dad right in the eyes and uttered, "Well"—he let a deep breath out and then—"we're pregnant."

Shock came first. Then silence. My parents were wide-eyed without the faintest hint of support.

Mickey explained that he loved me and wanted to marry me. He explained that he would make sure I was loved.

More silence.

We both apologized for disappointing them.

Oh, that deafening silence. It seemed eternal.

We began to talk about our plans, but that all seemed futile until they spoke. So we just waited and waded in the waters of the deepest silence I've ever known. I imagine now in that silent space was the most epic spiritual battle for my soul, for my marriage, for my children, for a legacy of love. It had to have been happening then because we needed one final victory. I had been in prison for too long. Jesus had the power to release me, but I had to want to leave. The enemy knew it, and he was doing everything possible to keep me there: barricading doors, powering down the lights, making it cold and damp, trying to kill me there while I held my head in shame.

During this eternal silence, I began to shake. Pride wanted me to walk out the door, acting flippant about their blessing and forgiveness. I almost did just that: walked out the door. My parents just looked at each other from across the room. They choked up. Tears welled up in their eyes. My head swiveled, waiting for someone to say something. I desperately wanted my mom to speak first. I knew she wouldn't lead with anger. She would hide disappointment and react with compassion. With my dad, I knew I'd hear the truth right away. I was afraid of what that might sound like.

"Please! Say something!" my soul screamed.

Finally, my dad uttered his first words while we held our breath. "I've been on both sides of this conversation, and I'm not sure which is worse."

Oh, the truth can be unbearable at times. I deserved it, though.

He continued, "Erin, this is not how we would've wanted you to start your life together, but we love you. We welcome you to the family, Mickey. We can't wait to meet our newest grandbaby."

*What? That's it?*

I was shocked. Silence pervaded the room while tears rolled down my cheeks. My parents stood and made their way over to embrace us. I wept. I cried tears of sorrow and joy, tears of regret and hope, tears of pride and humility. My world was undone, turned upside down, made right at the feet of Jesus. Grace and love overwhelmed me so deeply that I couldn't understand it all. I could not conceive of this kind of love. I knew better than to do what I had done. They knew I knew better. Yet their love for me triumphed. They could've reacted so differently. Instead, they poured the same love and grace they'd received a time or two onto us. In that moment, my parents displayed the unconditional love of Jesus. I hurt them; I disappointed them, and they loved me anyway. They didn't quote God's Word; they lived it. They did what great parents do, what they had done so many times before, except this time, it deposited in my heart. They handed God's love to us. I realized that if my earthly father was gentle and trustworthy with my broken heart and with his words of acceptance and love, then how much more would my heavenly Father tenderly love and accept me?

> **Do you know what invaded my prison in that moment? Grace. Mercy. Jesus.**

I don't know how I didn't see it before.

And that was all and everything it took. *That* was it. The battle for my soul ended. Jesus had the victory over sin and death in my life. Do you know what invaded my prison in that moment? Grace. Mercy. Jesus.

Grace that I knew I wasn't worthy to receive but accepted as my own.

Mercy that withheld a judgment that I deserved.

And my sweet Jesus, who took those nails in his hands for me, at this moment, because he wanted me back. He wanted me to know the depths of his love for me. He wanted me to understand that however desperately I longed for freedom paled in comparison to how desperately he wanted me to be free from the sin that bound me.

So he had been waiting in that prison with bolt cutters, waiting for me to see him. He, who had always been with me, who would never leave me, who knew every shameful thing I had ever done. He was waiting for this moment too. He couldn't wait for me to show him my sin, to hold up my shackled hands so that he could cut the chains. And with all his power and love, he took those bolt cutters to my chains and *clang! Clang!* They were no more. And in that moment, his love, his sacrifice, and his forgiveness became personal. He became *my* Jesus, *my* Savior, *my* Lord, *my* Redeemer, *my* Rescuer all at once. I understood every song I ever sang. Every Bible verse I had ever memorized became alive in me. I had immediate and overwhelming faith in him. It meant I was forgiven. I was forgiven before I had even repented. All at once, I dropped everything I was holding, every burden, all the things I thought would satisfy me, and I never picked them up again. I was never the same, just like my friend the Samaritan woman. The truth set us both free.

> The woman replied, "Let me drink that water so I'll never be thirsty again and won't have to come back here to draw water."
>
> Jesus said, *"Go get your husband and bring him back here."*
>
> "But I'm not married," the woman answered.
>
> *"That's true,"* Jesus said, *"for you've been married five times and now*

*you're living with a man who is not your husband. You have told the truth."*

The woman said, *"This is all so confusing,* but I do know that the Anointed One is coming—the true Messiah. And when he comes, he will tell us everything we need to know."

Jesus said to her, *"You don't have to wait any longer, the Anointed One is here speaking with you—I am the One you're looking for."*

*All at once, the woman dropped her water jar* and ran off to her village and told everyone, "Come and meet a man at the well who told me everything I've ever done! He could be the Anointed One we've been waiting for." Hearing this, the people came streaming out of the village to go see Jesus (John 4:15–17, 25–30, emphasis added).

Hey, village, the rest of this story is my invitation for you to meet the man at the well who knew everything I'd ever done and still chose to love me with his life. He is the Anointed One our souls long for. Come see for yourself.

By the power of Jesus, may the testimony of this one sinner-turned-saint release revival in you.

## LET'S REFLECT:

When was the last time you were hurt, disappointed, or betrayed by someone? Did you extend grace and forgiveness to them? Why or why not?

When was the last time you hurt, disappointed, or betrayed someone else? Did they extend grace and forgiveness to you? Why or why not?

What is your story of redeeming grace? When did you first come to believe in the Savior who cleansed you of your sins?

If you haven't said this type of prayer before, I invite you to read the following prayer out loud and surrender your heart to Jesus.

Heavenly Father,

I recognize that my sin has separated us. I can do nothing to earn your forgiveness or your grace. I cannot get to you on my own. I know that you sent your one and only Son, Jesus Christ, to pay for the debt of my sin. I recognize him as my Savior. I believe that he died for me so that I might live in perfect relationship with you. I believe that on the third day of his death, he was resurrected so that sin would no longer have a grip on me. I receive and believe it. I thank you for my salvation.

In Jesus's Name. Amen.

Praise the Lord! Welcome to the family! Please let me know if you prayed this prayer for the first time! I would be honored to celebrate this great victory with you!

MY WEEPING MAY LAST FOR A NIGHT,

BUT YOUR JOY COMES WITH
EACH NEW MORNING

SO, I WILL SING.

**"SING"**

**VALLEY'S END**

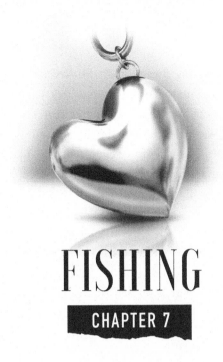

# FISHING

**CHAPTER 7**

As I sat down to write a chapter all about my husband, whom I love so deeply, I asked God, "Lord, what is it that you love so much about him?"

See, I know my words will fall flat compared to God's words of love toward him. Tenderly he answered, "I love the way he loves you." That couldn't be any truer. This man, my husband, loves me well. Each minute, hour, and day that I see him walk out this love toward me, I know more fully how deeply loved I am by my Savior. A husband's love toward his bride should be a reflection of Jesus's love for me and you, for us, his bride, the church.

Every movie made, every book written, every story shared of love reconciled, ought to invite us to a deeper understanding of how we've been reconciled to Christ. Even if it's a worldly understanding, our knowledge of Jesus will deepen the effect of the story as he reveals it to us. We don't have to disregard everything the world produces. We just put it under the glowing love of Jesus, let his truth and light reveal what the soul of human creativity yearns for: God's love is real.

After I had that life-altering dream about Mickey when we first kissed, we went to a football game together—because that just seemed to make sense—which was where we actually had our first kiss. In this sinful place we were living, we were both longing for something no earthly kiss, attention, drink, or physical experience could offer us. We tried to find it in each other for a year and a half of infidelity. By now, you've heard all the reasons why I was doing all this, but his reasons were different.

It would be so fun to have him write this chapter. You would learn the premise of his story in five hundred words, and he would leave you loving the simple and deep understanding of the redemption he has found. It's matter of fact and clear; there is no debating it. When he knows a truth, it is firmly planted in his heart and almost immediately becomes what the psalmist calls an oak of righteousness.

Once he received a bad cholesterol reading in his mid-twenties, mostly, I think because he had eaten McDonald's the day before. He didn't eat McDonald's for a year after that and only resumed eating there once every few weeks after his tests revealed that his cholesterol was back to normal. He doesn't stew over truth or process it like I do. Once truth is revealed he adopts it immediately. That's why I love him. He is one of the smartest, wisest people I've ever known.

He grew up with wonderful parents on five acres near the saltwater flats of Tampa as the youngest of three sons. His half-brothers were eight and ten years older than he was, so for all intents and purposes, he felt like an only child during his adolescent years. While his dad was laboring at the local steel plant, his mom worked at the family-owned community newspaper.

After school, Mickey would grab his fishing pole, tackle box, and a Snickers bar, and bike to the nearest available inlet. He'd fish for hours whenever possible. Some days, he was booted off the best spots, such as the railroad bridge, because they were supposedly off limits. Seriously? The railroad bridge? Had he never seen *Stand by Me?* Lord, help me.

Mickey loses awareness of anything else when he's fishing. He just comes alive in a new way. He looks like a kid having the time of his life, enjoying the creation that's been gifted to him. When he is fishing, the favor and hand of the Lord is upon him because he's just being himself. Gospel truth! In fact, one of our first real dates was deep sea fishing with his dad. I caught a couple of grouper but out of everyone on the charter, he caught a huge cobia. I grew to love him while spending hours and hours on the water with him.

When he was about fifteen, he started exploring activities that were a little more exciting than fishing. In a town where nothing ever happens, he grew bored with dropping a line in the water after school. He began goofing off at school, smoking and drinking a bit. Because of his upbringing, these weren't sins to him. They were either moral or amoral. You figured out which one based on the consequences, not by your love and knowledge of God. To Mickey, this stuff didn't have any spiritual consequences. That wasn't even a consideration.

During this time, his mom started having debilitating headaches. After a few visits to doctors, they found an inoperable, malignant tumor in her brain and cancer in her lungs. She was given a grim diagnosis of only six months to live. As they made plans for the end of her life, Mickey's world turned completely upside down. They spent time during her final weeks at a beach house near his grandmother's old cottage. His grandmother was a force for the kingdom of God. She swam in the ocean every morning. Her little white hair bobbed up and down in the current of the Gulf of Mexico while she prayed for her children, her grandchildren, and her great grandchildren.

In those final days, when Mickey wasn't fishing along the shoreline, he was listening to his mom pour out her wisdom, her stories, and the dreams she had for his life. She made him promise to go to college, to do more than she or his father had done.

Shortly after his sixteenth birthday, his mom went home to the arms of Jesus. Sometimes you tangle up a rope yourself. Sometimes, through no fault of your own, it gets handed to you all tangled up. Hopelessness and confusion come to us when this occurs without our faith in a sovereign God. That's where Mickey was. He had no faith, so whatever he was involved in just a bit before his mom's passing only escalated as he grieved and tried to sort through feelings he was never made to bear.

One early summer evening, he was laden and burdened with the emotion and weight of losing his mom. He went to the place where he had spent so much time, the shore of the beach on the west coast of Florida. He was just a few steps away from where he had last seen his mom enjoying her life. He plopped down into the sand. As the grains wrapped around his feet and funneled through his toes, he bowed his head and wept.

This posture, he couldn't have known, was just the place where hope was interceding. In that moment, words from his cousin came to mind. "You need to be saved." While Mickey's family only went to church on special occasions, his cousin was involved in a local youth group and had been saved. Whenever he saw Mickey, he told him about Jesus. Still, Mickey didn't know what being saved meant. Only heaven can tell us the depth of the salvation offered to us. As those words surfaced, Mickey cried, "I don't know if you're real, but if you are, I need you." In that moment, the peace that is beyond comprehension overwhelmed him.

I've heard him share this story over and over again. He always says the same thing. "I didn't know God yet, but I knew he knew me, and because of that, I just knew everything would be okay."

Mickey stopped the partying and started studying instead. His dad, who worked six days a week, took him fishing on his day off instead of to church. That was the most healing thing for both of them at the time. God met them there on the water each week. He didn't start going to church until we were married. I hadn't heard the story of God's intervention in his life; I didn't even know if he believed in God before we got married.

One night, after we found out we were pregnant, in the midst of all my panicked prayers about our future together, I had a jolt of remembrance. I grew very serious and explained to Mickey that I knew I was called to missions at a very young age. I knew that was still somehow part of God's plan for me although I didn't know how or if God would still use me. But I wanted to give Mickey the courtesy of knowing what he was signing up for if we got married. Aside from five weeks of premarital counseling videos, that was the only discussion we had about God's hope for our future. (Disclaimer: I don't recommend following this path!)

**As those words surfaced, Mickey cried, "I don't know if you're real, but if you are, I need you." In that moment, the peace that is beyond comprehension overwhelmed him.**

Then one day more than a year into our marriage, while sitting in church, the preacher talked about his own story of salvation. He explained, "Each of us should have a personal day, a date, a moment that we can point to as the time we came to believe." He made an invitation for those that hadn't had a moment like that yet. I was closing my eyes, hoping Mickey would raise his hand, hoping this would be the day. When we got in the car, I asked him about the message, wondering if he had raised his hand or if he'd had his own moment of salvation. He told me the story I just told you. But he said, "You know, I didn't know that was what had happened until today."

With that statement, I cried in the front seat of our car, in the traffic of a Sunday service exit, remembering the words my mom had spoken about my future husband. God had his hand on Mickey. I had prayed for him like she told me to when I was young. It swiftly and mercifully occurred to me that our sweet Lord had always known that Mickey would be my husband. It was as if he was saying, just like my dad said, "It's not the way we would've wanted you to start your life together, but we love you." In that moment, I realized that my husband knew and had experienced the loving embrace and peace of Christ. That was the beginning of what our God is having us do even now. It was the start of a new chapter. And to mark the new chapter, some weeks later, Mickey and I were baptized together, leaving our old life behind, surrendering fully to his plan, and declaring a new future in Christ.

This allowed us to start dreaming about what God had for us *together*. It was as if Jesus were inviting us to go fishing with him. This kind of invitation from our heavenly Father was perfect because I love being out on the water, metaphorically or literally, with Mickey. He is gifted and knowledgeable. He's at ease and challenged by the life around him. I forget about everything else when we're out there.

Since we've been together for over a decade, I've become familiar with the fishing day routine. Here's how it plays out:

❑ Wake up super early.

❑ Pack a cooler with sandwiches, drinks, and Snickers bars for quick eating. No bananas. They are bad luck for a reason neither he nor his father will explain.

❑ Grab the tackle, the cooler, the towels, sunscreen, bug repellant, and coffee (*because it is sooooo early!*)

❑ Head out to the water to find the bait.

❑ Watch husband maneuver the boat and cast the net.

❑ Marvel at his ability to multi-task because this is the only place it happens.

❑ Attach just-caught bait to the fishing line and cast.

Let me explain how cast nets work, in case you're not familiar with them. This type of net is like the proverbial wheel that can't be reinvented. The mechanics of it haven't changed much over the last couple of centuries. I'll try not to get too technical here. Picture a ginormous (technical term), round net with weights attached around the outside. This helps the net quickly sink into the water, trapping the fish. In the middle of this big net is a hole. Around the hole is a rope that wraps around the edge of the net and brings it into itself to capture all the lovely fish. To release the bait, you release the cap on the hole and shake out the catch. Then do it again, or don't, if you can catch all your bait in one cast, like my husband does every. single. time. Because he's a real fisherman who never misses a fish.

Now that we're all on the same page, I have to say, I love watching my man throw a cast net. I think the first time I actually saw him do it, I fell in love with him. The art of tossing the cast net takes practice, skill, and upper body strength that I don't possess, which is why I was so impressed. He knew this. I married him for it. He won.

Since we've had kids, this skillful handling is still impressive but for different reasons. Now I wrangle the kids while he rushes around the boat, watching, waiting, and anticipating the next move of his target. He's as agile as a cat, stepping over floaties and snacks, squirt guns and flip-flops.

Wow, babe.

We all wait while he works because we know the best part is about to happen: he stands as close to the edge as he can, with one end of the net between his teeth, and tosses it out onto the water. We all watch the net sink just below the surface.

Right about this time, my kids rush to the side to see if he caught any bait or if he needs to try again. Pardon me, I forgot, this never happens. Shall we continue?

We're all eager to know what's in the net, how many there are, and how big they are. He releases the fish, and the kids watch them flop all around the boat, count them, sometimes name them, trap them with their hands, and then throw them into the live-well. It's a lot of excitement after a bit of anticipation.

Why am I giving you this education on cast nets and fishing? Because Jesus called his first disciples, Peter and Andrew, right as they were casting their nets into the water. As you can imagine, this is not an ideal time for instructions or an invitation for any kind of fisherman.

"As Jesus was walking beside the Sea of Galilee he saw two brothers, Simon called Peter and his brother Andrew. They were casting a net into the lake, for they were fishermen. 'Come, follow me,' Jesus said, 'and I will make you fishers of men.' At once they left their nets and followed him" (Matthew 4:18, NIV).

At. Once. They left their nets.

Now the Bible doesn't tell us if the fishing was good that day, but I imagine it was. Jesus asks us to leave everything to follow him. "Everything" to them would've been great fishing. But even if this weren't the case, the very last thing any fisherman wants to do after he casts a net on the water is to release it before he sees what it holds, whether fishing is a hobby or his livelihood. In other words, he doesn't want to walk away from his fishing pole when he feels a tug on the line.

How do I know this? Y'all, I've seen my supernaturally patient and steady husband drop his sandwich in the water, spill his drink, knock over small children, and steal the rod out of my hand. And—I don't blame him for this one—he once almost ran into a piling when the fishing started to turn into actual catching. It just doesn't make any sense to leave your line or your net in the water and walk away.

But that's just what the disciples did. That's what Jesus asks us to do too—leave it all, because there is nothing on the other side of curiosity better than his love.

My favorite part of this story is when he says, "I will make you fishers of men." I wish I knew what they were thinking when he said that. I imagine it was something like, "Ummm . . . he said something about fishing so that sounds like fun. I don't know what the heck a fisher of men is, though." <Shrug>

**Jesus's gift to all his disciples is this: when we follow him into the boat or onto the shore, we catch sight of him and all he offers.**

In that moment, they had no other instructions. They were simply given an invitation to an unknown adventure, and they accepted it right away without waiting to see if something better would come along.

That significant Sunday after church, as Mickey understood the hand of God on his life, we both knew that we had been released and invited too. Just like Peter and Andrew, God's invitations can often seem vague to me, so I just have to lay down my perhaps agenda and follow him. Equally, his invitations are always intriguing, so I won't delay. What I love most is they are woven into what I'm already doing or something that I already love, something I'm gifted with, so I will pursue them with passion. Like the disciples, I just couldn't imagine at the time what more they could be fishing for than what was right in front of them.

Here's what I've learned. It doesn't matter what you're fishing for when you're fishing. It matters that you catch something. Jesus's gift to all his disciples is this: when we follow him into the boat or onto the shore, we catch sight of him and all he offers.

Many years later, we made a huge catch! Our oldest daughter was nine years old when she decided to be baptized. Our church had a baptism beach day coming up, and she wanted to proclaim her decision of faith. We stepped out into the water after a prayer on the sand. The water was perfect as she held her nose, awaiting the washing away of her sins once and for all. We stood on either side of her and echoed Jesus's words. "We baptize you in the name of the Father, the Son and the Holy Spirit. Buried in the water as Christ was in the grave and raised to walk in newness of life." We dipped her into the saltwater and out she came. New.

It didn't even dawn on us until we came out of the water that this was, in fact, the very same spot where Mickey's grandmother had swam all those years before. It was the very same shoreline that she had walked as she prayed for the generations of her children to know, love, and serve the Lord. Just forty yards away was the sandy patch where my husband had bowed his head in surrender, for salvation, for more than he could even imagine.

If I tried, I couldn't weave a more elaborate story of love, devotion, promise, or redemption. And believe me, as I've told you, all I did in my past was weave stories. I didn't trust the greatest storyteller to tell a greater story than I could. I know better now. Thank you for your patience with me, Jesus.

## LET'S REFLECT:

Who do you know who prays for you? Text them, or better yet, give them a call and thank them. Before you hang up, pray for them.

Where have you found yourself, through no fault of your own, in a place of immense grief or despair?

What was your response?

When was the last time you felt peace? Peace is your inheritance and the Prince of Peace is pouring it out. Receive it, friend.

WHEN I'M IN THE VALLEY

AND ALL I FEEL IS SHAME

YOUR LOVE SURROUNDS ME

I COME TO LIFE AGAIN.

**"YOU OVERWHELM ME"**

**VALLEY'S END**

# FORGIVEN AND LOVED

**CHAPTER 8**

*Forgiven!*

A poem of insight and instruction, by King David

> How happy and fulfilled are those whose rebellion has been forgiven, those whose sins are covered by blood. How blessed and relieved are those who have confessed their corruption to God! For he wipes their slates clean and removes hypocrisy from their hearts.
>
> Before I confessed my sins, I kept it all inside; my dishonesty devastated my inner life, causing my life to be filled with frustration, irrepressible anguish, and misery. The pain never let up, for your hand of conviction was heavy on my heart. My strength was sapped, my inner life dried up like a spiritual drought within my soul. Pause in his presence.
>
> Then I finally admitted to you all my sins, refusing to hide them any longer. I said, "My life-giving God, I will openly acknowledge

my evil actions." And you forgave me! All at once the guilt of my sin washed away and all my pain disappeared! Pause in his presence.

This is what I've learned through it all: All believers should confess their sins to God; do it every time God has uncovered you in the time of exposing. For if you do this, when sudden storms of life overwhelm, you'll be kept safe. Lord, you are my secret hiding place, protecting me from these troubles, surrounding me with songs of gladness! Your joyous shouts of rescue release my breakthrough. Pause in his presence.

I hear the Lord saying, "I will stay close to you, instructing and guiding you along the pathway for your life. I will advise you along the way and lead you forth with my eyes as your guide. So don't make it difficult; don't be stubborn when I take you where you've not been before. Don't make me tug you and pull you along. Just come with me!"

So my conclusion is this: Many are the sorrows and frustrations of those who don't come clean with God. But when you trust in the Lord for forgiveness, his wrap-around love will surround you. So celebrate the goodness of God! He shows this kindness to everyone who is his. Go ahead—shout for joy, all you upright ones who want to please him! (Psalm 32).

Gladness, joy, wrap-around love: these were the promises that awaited me when I confessed my sins to the Lord. That too-good, God-sized love that freed me right in my parent's living room. Love that I'll never comprehend while I'm on this earth. Love that is still changing me from the inside out. Love that is wrecking my world. Love that is providing more than I could ever imagine.

Much awaited us in the future. I didn't realize how desperately I would lean on God's love in the coming years, months, weeks, and even days that were beyond that moment.

Inexplicably, just three days after I crumbled at the feet of Jesus in my parent's home, I suffered a painful miscarriage. I was eight weeks pregnant. It was devastating and difficult, and even as I remembered that awful night, I buried my head and cried again for the life I lost in the midnight hour over a decade ago. The tiny life inside me served an important purpose; he brought me to my knees, to truth, to reality, to freedom. Thank you, precious child. I am so grateful for your life. It was not wasted, and we will meet again one day.

As we waited at the hospital, sifting through questions and feelings, guess who was there with us grieving? My entire family and a couple of sweet friends. They opened their arms of acceptance and understanding again to bring comfort and hope, to share tears and prayers. Something I might have missed if I would've waited to tell them I was pregnant.

The following week, Mickey proposed in an elaborate display. Although I knew it was coming, I didn't know when or how he would ask. I was scheduled to go see a movie with some friends that evening for a girl's night out. I was still feeling sick and exhausted from the miscarriage and crazy week. I didn't want to go. They begged, knowing things I didn't. They stalled for as long as they could, and by the time I got home, somehow Mickey had still managed to work out every detail in time.

I opened a door to a path of rose petals. I'm not typically enamored with pomp and circumstance, but when a proposal is afoot, then I'm all in. This is where it all belongs. Love ought to be given in simple and elaborate conveyances. This was both.

My house looked like a florist had moved their shop right into my living room. There were one hundred—yes, one hundred!—long-stemmed roses in fifteen different vases. It smelled amazing. It looked unbelievable. He had cleaned out every red rose from every floral shop in town. I dropped everything at the sight. Stunned, I realized I had nearly messed up the most amazing proposal ever. As soon as he saw me, he teared up and led me to the couch where he proceeded to turn on the TV.

Stop. The TV? Now? Really?

Yeah, I wasn't sure where that was going either. *Get to the proposal already, buddy!* I wanted to scream. But what popped up on the screen made me lose my breath. It was some of our favorite songs and pictures of me or us, compiled into a slideshow. In between each one, Mickey gave a reason why I was the woman of his dreams: one hundred reasons in all! One hundred!

**I mean, who in their right mind would create such an elaborate proposal for a woman who had cheated on her husband multiple times?**

One said, "I love you because you give the world's greatest hugs!" It had a picture of me squeezing the face of a dear friend. Another read, "I love you because you know famous people." It contained a photo of a chance meeting of me and Joey Fatone from NSYNC. The one that grabbed my heart said, "I love you because you look good in hats." Ha! We swung between laughter and tears through all one hundred reasons. I was deeply humbled by his thoughtfulness and his love.

See, both of us knew we didn't deserve a second chance at this kind of love. We knew who we were, what we were capable of, and what love in our own hands looked like. Yet here we were, hoping that despite ourselves, this love would be different, that this marriage would be different. I mean, who in their right mind would create such an elaborate proposal for a woman who had cheated on her husband multiple times?

Jesus. Let me tell you what he did.

We find this story in John 8:1–11. In the middle of his day, in the middle of a lesson, in the middle of the temple, some religious scholars, the keepers of the law, dragged in a woman who had been caught cheating on her husband. They used the truth, God's own law, to condemn her, to attempt to bring her to a violent death. Surely, they assumed, Jesus would have no alternative but to agree and condemn her himself. They were testing him. How would he get out of this predicament without breaking the law he proclaimed to have written *with* the Father God?

The pulse of a skeptical crowd was of no concern to Jesus. He said nothing. And in a bold and unprecedented move, he bent down to write something in the sand with his finger. Jesus's reply is so epic and perfect. See, this wasn't the first time God had written with his finger. The very laws they were asking him to honor were written with the finger of his hand on a tablet to Moses thousands of years ago. The scholars, who were far from acknowledging him as the Son of God, were incited to anger. Knowing this, Jesus looked at them and said, "The man who has never had a sinful desire can throw the first stone at her." In this moment, he is reminding us that the miniscule, secret, sinful desires of even the most righteous, law-abiding priest would be enough to condemn him.

With that, Jesus went back to writing in the sand. What was he writing in the sand, you wonder? What a wonderful question! So glad you asked! There are so many brilliant, scholarly theories about this. But the truth is, the Bible doesn't answer this explicitly. Therefore, this will be my second question when I get to heaven. Once I get up from at-his-feet worship and in-his-arms worship and holding-tight-to-him worship and dancing-for-joy worship, then I'll ask.

What I gather from my own study and my own similar redemption is that he used the ground as a symbol of this earthly kingdom too. There are two kingdoms: the kingdom of man and the kingdom of heaven. Jesus's life and death bridged the divide between them. For the incarnate God to write in the dust of the earth meant that he was trying to tell them something important about the two kingdoms. My guess was that his own finger, the very finger the religious wanted Jesus to use to point out her sin and ultimately condemn her, was the one he used to usher in her redemption. This earthly kingdom, living under the curse of the garden, finds fault in itself and accuses us. When we submit to the kingdom of heaven and the inheritance offered, there is no longer a charge against us. We are free.

I believe, with the full authority of the kingdom of heaven, in those moments, Jesus was writing all their names, knowing the sin that belonged to each of them. Sin which, under the law that they were hell-bent on serving, would condemn them, ostracize them, and eradicate them from their positions. But in this moment, Jesus was saying, if you want to live by this earth, you will die by this earth. This law won't do anymore. A new covenant is here. Your names, your life, won't be written in dust that will fade or wipe away or curse you. Your names can be written in my blood, tattooed on my hand, in a place that cannot be wiped away or blown away by the patterns of this world or by the works of your hands.

To me, Jesus was saying, "I'm after something far more valuable than what you do or don't do, what you've done or haven't done. I'm after your hearts."

Hebrews 7:19 tells us that the law was written to bring us to grace. That's exactly what happens here. These religious men were the keepers and protectors of the law, and they brought her to Jesus for correction, admonition, condemnation, and punishment. But what they all found was grace. His grace wasn't just for her; it was for them too. But they were too busy judging her sin to look at their own need for the same grace that was being offered to her. I think they saw their own names along with hers and departed. The very scandalous grace of Jesus levels the playing field of our sin.

Truly, Jesus would be the only one who had never and would never have a sinful desire. He was the only one who could hurl condemnation and stones at her and at them. But his mercy triumphed over judgement. It always has. It always will.

That kind of grace frustrates and confuses those who cling to religion, to the law, to the steps, to the rituals, to the sacrifices. That was the reaction of the men who brought the adulteress to Jesus. They left guilty from the oldest to the youngest. I bet she felt convicted, too, but her conviction drew her heart to repentance, as godly sorrow does. I think she saw her name along with theirs, those great leaders of the church, and had a completely different understanding: that all have sinned and come short of the worthiness of God's presence, until and if we believe.

**This law won't do anymore. A new covenant is here. Your names, your life, won't be written in dust that will fade or wipe away or curse you.**

In that moment, Jesus gave a proposal, an offer she would be silly to pass up. A gift we would all be foolish to reject: "Go, and from now on, be free from a life of sin." (See John 8:11.) It was as much an invitation as it was a declaration over her life.

Now why would Jesus invite and declare a life free from sin for her if that weren't possible? He wouldn't. I still don't think I can grasp this intellectually, but in my spirit, I know it's true. Just like this adulteress, the moment I repented, the moment grace crushed my sin, Jesus was giving me the same opportunity to go and from now on, be free from a life of sin.

To his proposal and to Mickey's, I said, "Yes!"

We were married five weeks later.

I can't imagine how my parents could go through all of my crazy and still happily walk me down the aisle and bless me just five weeks later. But that's exactly what they did.

My dad and I were arm in arm, just as we had been almost five years earlier, and he was about to release me into another covenant. Questions were swirling for him. Questions he would be sure he asked this time. Unlike him, I didn't have any reservations. I had released the reigns. I wasn't getting married because I was pregnant or ashamed or trying to make something right. I was getting married because I loved this man. God had provided a way for us to be restored to him in only five weeks' time. How could I not trust God in all his sovereignty?

I had to trust him because he was making a way out. He was bringing us out of the desolate land into his promises. I could feel it before I could see it, and everything I could see seemed too unbelievable to think it came from me.

As my dad asked me, "Are you sure this time?" I could only answer with a joyful and almost laughable certainty, "Yes. I'm so sure." My assurance wasn't in Mickey. Although he is as close to perfect as the Lord could give me, I know he is fallible. My trust was in Jesus. And in Jesus, I could begin to believe that his plan was starting to take shape.

My wedding day was filled with joyful anticipation. The Restorer was trading my ashes, all the things I had burned to the ground when they were in my hands, for beauty. I had picked up the ashes and given them to him as a humble offering. This was all I had. What could he possibly do with it? It still seems impossible. But our God delights in the impossible.

He is most known by us there. That glorious day, he breathed on Mickey and me and made something new. The joy and promise that was presented on February 18, 2007, was what every girl dreams to have on her wedding day. The hope was palpable. God's promises were true. Blessed assurance. He had great plans for me. He would build something enduring out of the rubble.

Fewer than fifty people were present to witness our tears as we exchanged our vows nearly twelve years ago as of the release of this book. It was a Sunday afternoon in the middle of February. It was the coldest and windiest day of the year and our wedding ceremony was to be held outside on the shore of Sanibel Island, Florida.

The director came to us in a tizzy, wanting to move it inside. It seemed like a simple request, but I realized with that decision to do what was best for us. I wasn't overly concerned with or neglectful of the guests at our celebration. We could consider their desires in accordance with ours because my eyes were fixed on different things now. I had grown up a bit. I didn't need things to be perfect. The weather wasn't worth my focus or my emotional investment. I couldn't change it, and we just couldn't compromise on the priority of an outdoor wedding. But we moved it to a place outside that was a bit more sheltered from the wind and elements. We shifted.

This was a stark contrast to all the fixin's I had ordered the first time I was married. The second time around, only a handful of people knew the song my sister sang so beautifully during our ceremony. We each only had one attendant beside us while we exchanged our vows in front of my brother-in-law, who performed our ceremony. My older sister said a beautiful prayer before our reception began, and we opted for a caricature artist over a photo booth. My dress was very simple, so I chose a beautiful veil that was eight feet long. But with the wind at its worst of the year, an eight-foot veil could be problematic and downright annoying. Somehow the veil was too important to leave behind. My mom attached it to my hair, and I let it fall behind me, not worrying about where it might go. I knew better than to chase the wind or the veil that blew in the wind. It was freeing and delightful. In all my outdoor pictures, my veil is swirling around us, adding height and depth to every photo and pose.

Even now, when we look back at those photographs, we are reminded that the wind truly made our day all the more memorable. We chose to pose for hilarious wind-blown pictures instead of stressing and trying to get the perfect shot. Somehow, in the excitement of our love, we knew we would find greater joy in the wind by dancing in it. I was set free to enjoy it all, no matter the circumstance. That's the way love works: it changes our perspective when we let it if we keep our eyes focused on it.

Over the years, the love that abounded from my father and mother, the head of my family, down to us created a sacred space for us to understand grace and truth. This occurred because of the relationship and discipling built over time. If love was the way for us to find forgiveness, then their relationship with us was the asphalt that made the path easier to follow. They forged the road for us, which eventually enabled us to share the entire sordid history of our relationship with them. We told them all about our eighteen month affair, my moments of indiscretion, and how we lived a lie for so long. My parents led us through healing and helped us break down strongholds, lies, and wrong agreements that came from the depth of our sin. They have forgiven us. They've showered us with grace and love. They've poured it over us from the well that never runs dry. Unbelievably, they've championed our story these many years.

From them, we've learned that love is best forged in deep relationships; it's meant to live there, which is why it takes time. Even though the people you love, who love you back, are messy, broken, and hurting, focusing on the love that binds you keeps you safe from the wind. The vows I said all those years ago are words that still ring true, that I still believe, but the weather has changed over and over and over again. Focus on the vows, not the weather.

C.S. Lewis says it this way:

> And, of course, the promise, made when I am in love and because I am in love, to be true to the beloved as long as I live, commits me to being true even if I cease to be in love. A promise must be about things that I can do, about actions: no one can promise to go on feeling in a certain way. He might as well promise never to have a headache or always to feel hungry.[6]

I knew this better than most. Remaining faithful in my marriage would require me to establish some new beliefs, to deal with some real issues, and to take some intentional steps with the Healer so that I could be the person Jesus and I wanted me to be. This has not been an easy road. If it were, then we'd be at the end of this book. I would triumphantly tell you that with forgiveness, everything was okay. Indeed, that is true, and yet somehow, God in his sovereignty allows us to meet defeat and foes that will require us to come to him, to ask for his help, to bring us to victory in a new way, to defeat our enemies, to surrender our feelings for the sake of his truth, and to love the people who seem to be our enemies. It is all for our healing and for his glory.

## LET'S REFLECT:

What does elaborate love look like to you? Have you ever been the recipient of it? Have you ever given it to someone else?

What do you know about the law of religion under the old covenant that condemns? What do you know about the law of love that forgives under the new covenant?

AND WHEN I GO UP THE HILL I SEE

YOUR ARMS WIDE OPEN

I SEE YOU RUNNING WITH LOVE FOR ME

TO HEAL WHAT'S BROKEN.

**"COMING HOME"**

**VALLEY'S END**

# HARD LOVE

**CHAPTER 9**

When we're going in and coming out of sin, just like the adulteress that was brought to Jesus, you can be sure a mob of people will find you. I just pray it's a different kind of mob than the one that found her. Mickey and I hadn't yet discovered who we were in Jesus. We didn't know yet what he said about us. We were just beginning to understand our identity. God's grace is such that we don't have to be perfect in our understanding of his teachings. In fact, even in the midst of sorting our imperfections, Jesus says we still get to be the carriers of his perfect love. And how much better when we feel the perfect love of Jesus through imperfect people? It's supernatural. That supernatural love is what pulled me out of all my sin. This love stood in stark contrast to the Pharisees who pulled out the woman caught in adultery. (By the way, where was the dude who was with her? Was he not guilty of breaking God's law too? Maybe I'll save that topic for another book.)

Supernatural love filtered through the hands of those imperfect people smelled my funk and embraced me anyway. Love expressed through my family and friends has taken their time, their resources, their sleep, their food, and their homes. It has required an emotional, physical, and spiritual investment into my life. It cost them something. They shared grace as if they had too much of it. They let me question things about the Bible and God's love as if Google didn't exist. They let me ugly cry all over them as if they were my pillow. They let me angry fight for forgiveness. They let me work through disappointment and confusion. Here we are, years later, and here they are still. Man, I can't believe they still call me! But they do. They still cheer. They still know all that yuck. I'm still their friend anyhow. They still love me.

After all this loss, I found myself at the bottom of a deep cave. That's when my Savior and my family that loves like him came in and wove me a rope of grace. They saw all the filth I was standing in and still tethered themselves to me; they locked themselves into the mountain of God's love, secured their stance, and helped me climb out of the darkness I was in. His love, the truth, and acceptance pulled me out of the lies and secrecy and into the light. So much darkness remains in well-kept secrets; it's so rarely exposed to the light. With each step, I surrendered my desire to mask the imperfections of my abilities and ugliness of my soul. And my climbing crew watched and cried and cheered and encouraged and cared for me with every pull.

"Tolerate the weaknesses of those in the family of faith, forgiving one another in the same way you have been graciously forgiven by Jesus Christ. If you find fault with someone, release this same gift of forgiveness to them. For love is supreme and must flow through each of these virtues. Love becomes the mark of true maturity" (Colossians 3:13–14).

Love did that for me. People filtering perfect love through their own sinful hands did that. My own personal growth and walk with my Savior did that.

But it required something of me: vulnerability. And it required something of them: acceptance. We don't necessarily like either of those things. Our own vulnerability and that of others can often scare us. Acceptance of others requires us to accept our own shortcomings, which requires us to be honest with ourselves, which requires—you guessed it—vulnerability.

See, it wouldn't have been enough for my parents to guide me through inviting Jesus to reign in my heart if they walked away from me when I forgot to live that way. As the Body of Christ, we can't do that either. The beauty of surrender is found in both the first moment of surrender and in the continued faithful walk of surrender. As believers, we must value both equally.

In Romans, Paul has some important instructions on how to love each other within the family of God. He teaches us in such a way that it leaves us with no option but to love in the reckless way Jesus loves us still, the way my family chose to love me—without quitting on each other when things got uncomfortable.

> "Be devoted to tenderly loving your fellow believers as members of one family. Try to outdo yourselves in respect and honor of one another" (Romans 12:10).

That word devoted, *phileostorgos*, translates into a compound word with two definitions of love as given by the Greeks. The first half is *phileo*, which means brotherly love, mutual respect, and admiration for one another. It is easily given because it's a mutually beneficial relationship. It's reciprocal. The second half is *storge*.[8] This is the kind of love that a parent feels for a child; siblings feel it for one another too. It's a protective and almost an obligatory kind of love. It's the kind of love that can take a beating and still give because its basis is found within our very DNA.

The only place in the Bible where these two words are combined is in this verse in Romans. How annoying. I know. I want to scream, "Anywhere but here, Lord!"

I'm guessing that even though I'm hilarious, wise, and super humble, it *maybe* hasn't always been easy for people to love me. How tragic! I use myself as an example here because I am acutely aware that church people are hard to love because we think they/we ought to know better. And if I'm professing that, then I, just as well as anyone, need to be lumped into that statement.

**Paul is teaching the Romans—and is still teaching us—that unadulterated love is the only way the family of God thrives.**

Hi. I'm Erin. And I'm not always easy to love.

But there is no mistake in Paul's positioning of this verse. This is where it absolutely belongs. Paul is teaching the Romans—and is still teaching us—that unadulterated love is the only way the family of God thrives.

Listen, I genuinely and truly love my brother and two sisters. They are the first people I call in any kind of crisis and in every kind of celebration. They are heroes of faith to me. Their kids are like my own. Their spouses are cherished family members I deeply respect and admire. Our get-togethers make up my favorite memories. We did not come into this earth with that kind of love. We had to be taught to love each other with kindness. We had to learn to share and speak love toward each other. Who does that at the age of two without instruction? No one. That, my friends, is phileo love.

On the other hand, even at two years old, we didn't have to learn to shut somebody up if they messed with one of our own. If my little sister was shoved, protection for her rose up in me instantly. That's storge love.

When I was in fifth grade, my brother, a six-foot-four senior in high school, would walk me home after class. I would tell him about the joys and hardships of my day, and inevitably he would ask, "Need me to beat anybody up next time I pick you up?" I knew he meant it. I knew that if there was a threat to me, my brother would come in and handle it. While my brother was ready to beat somebody up, my big sister took an alternate route. She would stick her pointer finger in the face of anyone who dared to look at me wrong and ask one defiant question, "You want to mess with me?" It was as much said with her stance and expression as it was with her words. Anybody willing to go through those two must've seriously had a beef with me. Our sweet youngest sister had one more to contest with if anyone dared hurt her, and that was me. It didn't matter if any of us had gotten into a fight with each other moments before; if protection was needed, protection was given. Paul is beckoning the church to that kind of family love. But it's more than just protective love Paul is referring to here.

I have been asked this question many times in my life, "Is your family close?" The answer is yes, we are very close. But close doesn't mean we are ignorant to each other's weaknesses. We aren't blissfully unaware. We simply *choose* to love beyond a protective love. We choose to live and love like we have a choice whether to be friends. We choose to accept one another's flaws and to encourage growth, to be inconvenienced for the sake of the other, to pray when words fail us, to reach out when the need arises, to find joy in time spent together, and to keep invitations extended. No matter what.

My brother said the most wonderful thing to me one day when I invited myself to a celebration he was having. He said, "Erin, I don't ever want to be in a place where you're not welcome."

Man, me too.

Please, let this become the cry of your church, Lord.

And I know. It's hard to love the people who

- ❏ make really stupid choices
- ❏ don't do things like we would
- ❏ don't smell right
- ❏ don't look right
- ❏ are awkward or have terrible social skills
- ❏ are too emotional
- ❏ don't want help
- ❏ have a sordid past or
- ❏ have a sordid present.

I was that hard-to-love person. I have a feeling you might be too.

After Mickey and I exchanged the promises and came back from the honeymoon, we found out we were pregnant once again. We arrived at the reality of relationships that needed more healing. Turns out the forgiven adulteress had to go somewhere after she left Jesus, too, in order to deal with the consequences of her decisions. Same for us. Trust had been broken with friends, co-workers, and family. We knew it would require us to love like Jesus did.

While the revelation of the saving grace of Jesus is an instant and overwhelming experience, living outside those chains is a process. It takes time to navigate how to cross from one side of the wilderness to the other side of the promised land. Ask the Israelites. Ask Peter. Since God lives outside of time, he is not rushed for our sakes. The process of renewal is where he shines. He doesn't hurry us up even when we're desperate for him to move it along. We're afraid it will hurt. We're afraid it will break us.

When my kids need medicine or a Band-Aid or stitches removed, you'll never find me nearer and quieter with them then as the medicine is being administered; the stitches are being sewn, or the Band-Aids are being removed. On their own, without me, they would never agree to these remedies. They would fight against them because they can't comprehend that something that hurts for even one second would bring about healing.

As a new mom, when our first daughter was just a year old, we took her up to Maumee Bay State Park in Ohio for my cousin's fall wedding. It was chilly, and she had been wearing her adorable little mittens all week. She was getting grumpier as the days went on, and we assumed it was because of the traveling and late nights. As I was bathing and dressing her for the wedding that Saturday afternoon, she was whining and clenching her fists. I sat her in my lap to do her hair, and as I looked over her shoulder, I detected little specks on the palm of her hand. She was eating her snack, and as she grabbed another little rice puff, I spotted more specks. I could tell something was off, so I brought her up to me on the bed with her face near mine. I held her hands gently, brushing them open with my fingers. She had no less than twenty little wooden splinters freckling both of her chubby little hands. I freaked out, wondering how I had missed this. Many of them were red and deep, indicating they had been there for a while. I felt like I was the worst mom ever for not recognizing her pain over the last few days.

I grabbed her mittens and saw that those fleece things we kept making her put on were laden with even more shards of pain. Several days before, she had been playing on a wooden deck that ran along the perimeter of the property. Moving her hand back and forth over wooden planks with fleece gloves on was like pulling pins up with a magnet. Her mittens attracted every tiny loose fragment of wood. Each time we put them back on her, more would find a home in her hand.

As I cried with Mickey in our hotel room, I realized I had no idea what to do. We were far away from our pediatrician, and the wedding was in two hours. I knocked on the door of my mom's room, telling her the news and asking for her wisdom. She said, "Take care of your daughter first." She told us to go to the nearest hospital and not worry about disappointing anybody at the wedding. We arrived at the hospital, frantic and praying. They called us back, and we were met with two angels, I'd bet. The two paramedics on call that day were both fathers of young daughters. As they lovingly assessed her hands, they told us the best way to help her would be to keep her still and lying down with her hands strapped down to her side so they could each work on one hand at the same time. This would be the most efficient way to remove the splinters, but it would still feel like a very long process to her.

They both ended by saying, "If it were my daughter, this is how we would do it."

We agreed to their plan and let them strap down her hands. They began to speak calm words over her, calling her by name, never raising their voices, even when she was crying loudly. I put my face next to her head, wiped her tears away, and sang her a song. As I did, she began to calm down. They hadn't even pulled out the first splinter yet. I wasn't sure I would be able to endure the next thirty minutes. If she moved even a little bit, she could suffer more pain. And some of those splinters were buried deep in her skin. It would take a bit of peeling back to remove them. The angels continued to pull out the pieces while I sang to her, and reminder her about the lollipop she would certainly get when she was done. The thirty minutes rolled by, and all forty or so splinters were removed. Healing antiseptic was applied before they wrapped her itty-bitty hands in bandages. They released her from the straps that held her down, and we all celebrated what was sure to be an easy recovery now, especially with the introduction of the lollipop.

From the hospital, we went straight to the wedding reception.

I found myself in this same place after Mickey and I were married. It was as though my hands were still hurting from what I had done. Some splinters—shame, fear, insecurity, and others—needed to be removed from my life. Thankfully, some angels, including my mom and dad, knew what they were doing; they helped me heal. They have been tender and kind, a real reflection of Jesus. They reminded me from their own experience of what awaits if I will yield to the tough stuff right now.

It took a while for my parents and I to fully heal. Just like I grieved when I realized I didn't notice how long my sweet girl had been in pain, playing with clenched fists, my parents also knew that they had done things that led to my pain. It grieved them. During this time, we discovered that all of us needed to seek forgiveness from each other and from the Lord for the role we played in causing each other pain. It turns out this love to which Paul implores us only works where truth and forgiveness dwell.

Funny thing is, in our minds, when we consider going through a process like this, we believe it will scar us instead of heal us. But when done through and with humility, the process heals the wounds beautifully. See, we aren't meant to suffer for suffering's sake; we're meant to suffer like Jesus did for love's sake—the kind that restores, heals, and builds trust.

**It was as though my hands were still hurting from what I had done. Some splinters—shame, fear, insecurity, and others—needed to be removed from my life.**

For a while, Mickey and I attended the church where I had gone with my ex-husband. We realized quickly that some people felt like those splinters could never be removed and my wounds were permanent. They seemed to think it served me right for doing what they correctly assumed I had done. Unlike my family, their embrace wasn't so grace-filled. They needed to believe in a God who dispensed judgement over forgiveness, or better yet, forgiveness with dire consequences, such as withholding the love of God's people. That was a sure-fire way, they guessed, to keep me from doing anything like that again. We soon realized this was not a healing place for us. Staying there would prolong our pain, which would be suffering for the sake of suffering.

It took time to find a safe refuge where people cared about our injuries and our healing more than they cared about all the juicy details of how we came to be injured. Eventually we did, and once healed, these folks cared enough to point us in the direction of the blessed wedding Jesus had invited us to.

After my daughter was bandaged, holding tightly to her lollipop, we checked the time and realized we had completely missed the wedding ceremony. We would, however, be right on time for the reception.

For Mickey and I, when we made those vows to each other, we certainly didn't understand—and still don't understand—some keys to loving each other forever. How crazy is it that after a wedding, we are invited to celebrate promises that we can't possibly, rightly, and fully understand? That's where forgiveness leads. That is the kingdom of God. He beckons, won't you come to the party? Let's unwrap those gifts and learn how to use them together. Let's celebrate the gifts and promises that you can't comprehend.

## LET'S REFLECT:

Does the modern day church look like what I've described in this chapter? Why or why not?

What does a devoted community look like in practical terms?

How do you affect the change you long to see in the church?

Is there any broken place that you feel is too tender to touch, even if it's a healing touch?

I'M DONE WITH TALKING

NOW IT'S TIME FOR ACTION

FED UP WITH ARGUMENTS

'BOUT ALL MY RIGHTS

THIS SELFISH WAY OF LIFE

IS LOSING TRACTION

I'M READY TO BE ALIVE.

**"PLAYING IN THE SAND"**

**VALLEY'S END**

# KNEEL!

## CHAPTER 10

"Live every week like it's shark week." Mickey, the team leader at our real estate office, had started each day of our sales training with this moniker. It was a summons for all of us to keep alert, enjoy the exhilaration of not knowing all that's out there, dare to discover, and ironically, what it would mean for us, watch your back.

At the end of the presentation he had spent weeks preparing, he was tapped on the shoulder and shuffled into the office of our senior manager. I stewed in my heels as I sat outside the office and rubbed my five-month-pregnant belly. I heard the rumors swirling that others had been called into different offices, but all were discussing the same thing: layoffs.

I began to panic. What would this mean for him, for us? How could they do this? He just led the entire team in a sales training! Last we heard, he was being groomed for management. I felt betrayed. A yet-undiscovered emotion known as pregnant feisty rose within me. Put your dukes up, man. This is about to go down, and I *will* win because you can't hurt a pregnant lady. I was about to have an unapologetic, Jerry McGuire moment when Mickey walked out silently, bewildered and betrayed.

The car ride home was deafening. Our plans had been forged, carved out in the concrete caverns of our own minds, and now they were wiped away like yesterday's menu off a dingy chalk board. We weren't steady on our marriage feet or family feet or Jesus feet yet. And here we were, to make matters worse, standing on shaky career and financial ground.

I'll be honest, that first year of marriage in 2007 was a doozy. Even though he was asked to leave, I wasn't. I had to stay at the company, newly pregnant, awaiting my maternity leave and terrified of what life would hold now. The economy was kicking our real estate career keester, it turned out. We had moved into a recession and between the two of us, owned three houses. The situation certainly looked dire. At times, I thought maybe this was our punishment for all the mistakes we made. I let that guilt marinate for a little while on my fifty-minute drive to and from work every day. All those minutes turned out to be a great opportunity to weed stuff out of the garden of my soul.

We used to have a garden in our backyard. We grew all kinds of vegetables, herbs, and flowers. My kids and I learned well through this garden that we can't make anything grow, and we certainly can't make anything grow faster. As my girls would play outside, they would pull peas or green beans off the vine or carrots out of the ground when they were hungry. Once, to our horror, one of them mistakenly took a huge bite out of a jalapeno.

One perfect spring day, the girls were outside running around the yard and wanted to eat something from the garden. They moved through the beds, snapping off a pod of peas. Before I had a chance to intercept, they had already popped a few peas in their mouths. Have you ever eaten a pea too early? It's really hard and not very palatable. Each time they tested out the harvest, they quickly learned what wasn't quite ready for picking.

I'm still learning the beauty of the process as I wait for God to grow things in me, especially those creative things that are meant for human consumption, things that he wants us to share with other people. Your crop just won't be as beneficial if it's harvested too early. Give it time to grow.

In those early years, God was planting and tilling and watering the garden of our souls a lot. We had much to learn and unlearn about him. I carried old mentalities—these false beliefs and strongholds—into my new marriage.

**One of these was best expressed in my journal years before:**

*I heard this quote about character being a reflection of who you are when no one else is looking. I feel I haven't been able to share all the bad things in my life because I didn't think I would be forgiven or accepted. I hid everything bad or sinful in myself, which makes me think, What kind of character do I possess?*

I wish I could go back and shake myself. "You possess the very character of God!" I would exclaim.

I certainly wanted the Lord to hurry up and fix all the things I knew were still broken in me. There was so much that I had done wrong, so many people that I hurt, so much destruction that had come from my choices, and those choices had consequences. I had to rebuild trust in some of my relationships; I had to walk away from people who wanted me to be who I used to be. Even in my healing, I made a lot of mistakes. I still do, but once I started learning who I was, I began behaving differently. This would take something I hadn't practiced in many years: humility. From humility flows serving, giving, mercy, love, forgiveness, and grace.

It's not enough to say, "Come fill me, Lord, with all of you." We must first say, "Empty me of all of me so that I might be filled with all of you.

I am wholly yours." We must become less so that he will become more. Not because we hate ourselves but because we *love him.* He doesn't come at us with that kind of healing. He knows we scare easily. He has to let love gently lead us to repentance and healing. That's what he spent those morning and evening car rides doing.

C.S. Lewis wrote, "He cannot ravish. He can only woo."[9]

He woos us through grace. There is no fear or shame in humility, only a higher view of Jesus than yourself. The only way I could conceivably love my husband and not make a mess of my marriage again, the only way I could live unafraid of what the future would bring, was if I loved God first. I didn't know what it looked like to live my life without my own agenda, without being in control, without my boxes to check. I hadn't loved myself less than anybody . . . ever. It had been all about me for so long.

> **Humility is the key while we are on this earthly journey, and we should cling tightly to it.**

In middle school, one of the movies I watched repeatedly was *Indiana Jones and the Last Crusade.*[10] If you've never seen it, Indiana Jones is an archeologist on an epic search for the Holy Grail, the cup Jesus drank from at the Last Supper. His father, who is looking for it as well, is captured by men who also want the cup for the power it possesses. Their hearts are evil. Indiana Jones must uncover the clues and journey to where the Holy Grail lies and give it to the men as a ransom for his father's freedom.

His father is facing a life-threatening injury, needing only a sip from the cup to heal his wound. As he starts toward the path his father laid out for him, he heads into a dark section where men before him have gone and died. He echoes the words his father is praying behind him, "Only the penitent man will pass." Indiana Jones is repeating these words, trying to understand their meaning so that he can stay alive as well.

"The penitent man is humble before God," he remembers. "A humble man kneels before God. *Kneeeeeel.*" he exclaims, before dropping to his knees in an act that saves him from a prideful fall, decapitation, and death. Humility is the key while we are on this earthly journey, and we should cling tightly to it. We must scream *"Kneel"* to ourselves if we have to just to avoid the fall that will inevitably come with pride. The first step to partaking of God's cup of promise is humility.

In the tiny house where I grew up was a huge eat-in kitchen. While there was no island in the middle, above where an island could've conceivably sat was an old chandelier pot rack. It hung by a ring in the middle, which meant when you hung the pots, you had to stagger them evenly to balance them, or one side would hang low while the other nearly grazed the popcorn ceiling. As each of us grew taller, we had a moment or two of contention with this pot rack. We coined it *humility.* As we barreled into the kitchen, if the pots weren't hung right or if we had hit a growth spurt and weren't paying attention, we would inevitably knock our heads against a copper-bottomed pot. Like a cartoon scene, the bells of St. Mary would ring out in chorus with doves swirling around our heads. Whoever witnessed the humility would quip something like, "Pride comes before fall," or "Bend low before your God." Ya know, something that really sealed the lesson. It was always a hilarious metaphor for how cringe-worthy and also how revealing pride can be.

We hate to think that we bend toward pride or that it could possibly be found in our hearts, leaving less room for our Savior. But it happens. And it happens far more often than I care to admit. Because pride.

Wrestling with the unknown of a new family and no job during a recession that would certainly bring more layoffs in a declining real estate market offered a great opportunity for pride to ruin my faith.

Humility had to come; hope had to release; grace was provided; love had to cover, and faith had to be received. It filled in all the gaps between the wilderness desert and the promised land that had pierced the bridge that was the sacrificial life of Jesus Christ. Everything is buttoned up and answered perfectly through Jesus. He is the only way.

That's why grace is so confounding. It doesn't follow a logical path; it *fills* the broken path.

But oh, for the perfectionists, this is maddening. This is astonishing. We want the answers: this is how it works, this is where it comes in, this is when we'll find it. It's our deep need to know, to possess, to control, to rule. In our hearts, we want surprising, audacious, confounding, joyous, overwhelming grace. In our minds, we want logical and practical steps to righteousness. The answer is simple. It works when, where, and if you surrender all that.

The truth is real humility comes from a place of poverty, of being without— without your own knowledge, your own will, your own agenda, and your own understanding. It comes from a fully surrendered life.

In Matthew 5, Jesus's first teaching, the Sermon on the Mount, contains his very first words to us. Here, he proclaims our identity and speaks blessings over us. He, in fact, calls us blessed. But his words are so perplexing, and in this message, he goes about flipping every notion of prosperity on its head.

"Blessed are the poor in spirit, for theirs is the kingdom of heaven" (Matthew 5:3, NIV).

*The Passion Translation* notes:

"This word, blessed, is from the Aramaic word *toowayhon* meaning 'enriched, happy, fortunate, delighted, blissful, content, blessed.' Our English word *blessed* can indeed fit here, but *toowayhon* implies more— great happiness, prosperity, abundant goodness, and delight! The word *bliss* captures all of this meaning."[11]

The idea is that in order to live in this place of bliss, you must reach the end of yourself. In your longing for God, you realize that you do not possess the pieces and parts to get you into the kingdom, and from this place of poverty and surrender, you inherit the kingdom of God. This is humility, the most valuable posture in the kingdom of heaven.

Oswald Chambers writes:

> It takes us a long while to believe we are poor, but that is the entrance. The knowledge of our own poverty brings us to the moral frontier where Jesus Christ works.[12]

One night, a year or two after Mickey and I were married, I was driving home from Bible study. The Lord was working on me and showing me how I had lost my identity in him for all those years. Ever so gently he said,

"Erin, I know you don't want to go down that broken road again, so find yourself in me. As you take those steps toward me, you will have the marriage you desire; you will be the woman you want to be, the mom you want to be, the wife you want to be. And you and Mickey will grow more and more in love."

I surrendered and cried in my driveway that night as I realized I was beginning to fear that I would fall into old ways as I struggled in my new role as a mom. I was desperate to live my life openly and honestly, but I had no idea how to do it. I didn't understand it then, but whenever I made a mistake, I began to condemn myself. I had subtly begun to exchange my humility and grace for unworthiness and shame once again. Mom guilt is real, y'all.

Shame had placed a scarlet letter *A* on my chest like a sin super-hero. I was branded. "This is who you are, and if you forget, look in the mirror, and this will serve as a reminder." Yes, my chains of bondage had been broken, and I was out of prison by now. But I was still carrying the iron ball of shame. I didn't know how to release that shame, still acting and thinking like a prisoner.

**And so it wasn't until I came to the very end of my own reputation, my own desire to defend myself or my husband, or orchestrate my own version of peace with people, that I could release forgiveness...**

It was as if I had graduated from high school, with my diploma in hand, singing the chorus of hallelujah, freedom, yet I was still carrying around my backpack of books. What was the point? It was unnecessary and burdensome. The weight that I carried simply reminded me of what I had done. I couldn't accept all the freedom the diploma offered. Maybe I wouldn't have to show up for my high school classes anymore, but the weight constantly reminded me of the classes I had taken: the ones I hated, the ones I struggled with, the ones I failed, and even the ones I soared through. That weight tainted—even what should have been—great memories. Not only that, but I couldn't move ahead to the next step in my education and my future because of this burden.

That is what shame feels like. You *know* you're free. You just can't step into freedom.

Friends, I could not do a single thing to ever be worthy enough to receive the beauty of God's grace, but if I don't agree with him, with he who says I am worthy, then I render the cross useless for my sake. He didn't come to only offer forgiveness; he came that I would have fullness of life with him. That means taking all the truths of the gospel as my own.

And so it wasn't until I came to the very end of my own reputation, my own desire to defend myself or my husband, or orchestrate my own version of peace with people, that I could release forgiveness to those we felt betrayed us, to those who insulted us, to those who accused us, to those who hated us, and ultimately—and this is so important—to ourselves. Humility receives and releases love.

In that moment, the same forgiveness that I had known from Jesus was used to allow me to forgive myself.

And like a three-year-old child, *I* could suddenly say to the accuser, "Nah-uh, adulteress is not the name my Father gave me. As a believer, I am called a saint, a daughter, a co-heir with Christ. I'm his bride, his promise, his love, his friend. I am worthy to receive his name." And on that day, I realized that he had already exchanged my scarlet-lettered garment for a white dress.

I know he didn't free me from my former life just so that I could be married again or have children. He freed me so that I could know him because he desired me. My surrender invited him to remove every other affection in my heart because he knew what my heart craved was only satisfied in him. I couldn't love another well without knowing I was loved well by him. I first had to know that his promise was to love me, that his love would never change or fade, and that it wasn't indicative of his fluctuating mood. It was a promise that had been put into action thousands of years ago, so all the love I gave to Mickey in our marriage would be the fruit of a love tree that I had planted with Jesus first.

It's just as Jesus says in Matthew 6:33–34.

"Seek the Kingdom of God above all else, and live righteously, and he will give you everything you need. So don't worry about tomorrow, for tomorrow will bring its own worries. Today's trouble is enough for today" (NLT).

Yep, bestowing the love of Jesus toward a spouse—or anything or anyone else—is less important in the kingdom than first receiving and living in the love of Jesus. But once you love like this, you quickly realize that you can't have one without the other, and the results of living this way come immediately as the verses above say. I have been given a glimpse of God's love, and it is so bold and fierce that my mind, heart, and body cannot contain it. It is joy unspeakable! That is the realm of God's kingdom economy. It cannot make sense to our earthly minds; it has to be received by our spirit with faith.

Getting out of our own way shifted the tone of our marriage. As we sought out new jobs, we began to pray about what we desired: the job, the pay, and the schedule. We did it in humility and with intention. I wrote everything down. We didn't have an agenda, but we wanted to record the desires of our hearts so that we could see where they aligned with God's. We released our own plans and listened for his. We prayed over what we wrote down. These were our very first prayers as a married couple. It seemed to be important enough to pray about, so we trusted that God would direct us as we took those first tentative steps of faith with him.

I am convinced that those prayers we prayed, in the first two years of our marriage, both then and now, came from heaven to point us and one another back to heaven.

My life is still becoming the evidence of this great understanding. Two years later, five years later, ten and twelve years later, Mickey and I can look at the life and business we have now, knowing it was birthed in the surrender of our hearts to his will for us through those prayers. Every single one has been answered, not for our sake alone, but because our Father who is good and holy knew what he was doing from the beginning. We just had to trust him.

## LET'S REFLECT:

Mickey and I went through a huge upheaval when he lost his job. Have you ever found yourself in a similar situation? What did you cling to?

In what ways are you clinging to the fleeting things of this earth?

Where have you been saying, "Come fill me, Lord, with all of you" when he's first asking you to empty yourself of you?

What would you do if you weren't afraid?

ENJOY BEING YOU TODAY!

FILL THE LAND WITH HIS

PRAISES AND TRUTH! YOU ARE

AN ANSWER TO HIS PROMISES!

**MY MOM**

# CHILDREN

## CHAPTER 11

**My Girls**

The idea of balance is a hoax.

Take a short drive in any direction from our house to the nearest park, YMCA, aquarium, or theme park, and you will likely find a pretty epic outdoor splash pad. We live in Florida, so water features are necessary in many of our outdoor landscapes. One play space in particular boasts a giant sprayer that spills with force out of the top steel beam into a cone balanced on the point of its base. As the water fills the giant cone, the cone inevitably topples over and pours water into smaller basins, which spill into even smaller vessels, splashing over the sides and onto the sun-scorched kids below. Most of the kids are waiting for it, laughing in anticipation. But every now and then, an unsuspecting little one is both shocked and relieved by the rush of cool water on a hot summer day.

To me, this looks more like what Jesus wants our lives to reflect rather than some shadowy pursuit of balance. We have to sit under the fountain where we are filled up; then when the vessel cannot hold any more, it topples and spills out onto the ones closest to us. It then fills and refreshes the ones closest to them and pours out on the ones who need it most, the ones who are hot and thirsty.

As a vessel, we have to be empty to be filled up, to spill out. We can't take credit for the water, can we? Nope. And that's exactly how love gets bestowed to those around us too. They see our pouring out; they know that we aren't the line that feeds the water, so they move into position to be poured into by the Living Water instead of us. What a godly perspective!

The Bible tells us that the same is true for every other thing we pour into our lives. We are a cone balancing on a narrow, pointed base. If we haven't turned the water on or if we have moved away from the water, then something else will fill us. And when it does, we're going to tip over. The question for us is, what do we want to dump on other people and into the other little vessels around us?

My entire life as a mom has been spent inching myself closer to the main supply of water, the source of every good thing. I cannot do these hard tasks—cleaning toilets, attending a meeting, facing injustice, or writing a book—without a fresh release from the well that never runs dry. I have never felt more of a pouring from the source than I have in writing this book or giving birth to my babies. Funny thing, the process feels almost the same.

My first birth with Ella was at the hospital with an epidural. I felt nothing until afterward. Her entrance into the world was sweet and wonderful. It's weird how you can never have met someone, and yet when you meet them, it's as though your heart, your spirit, has known them forever. That's how I felt when I met her. I cried because of a rush of hormones and also because my soul was rejoicing, knowing that I was now seeing a part of my heart I didn't know existed. She was there in our arms, just barely six pounds, and I felt as if Jesus was right there with us. He was elated that we were finally meeting. He knew her. He knew me. He knew Mickey. In consideration of all time, people, and opportunity, he chose to put the three of us together right there. She was a celebration.

My second girl, Myla, was birthed at a birthing center about an hour from our house. I felt uneasy on the morning she was born. I didn't want to eat anything. All that I could do was just stand in the shower. It was my actual due date. When it comes to birthing babies, records show that they aren't usually on time. But my girl, Myla, is punctual and prepared and has been from the beginning. She was ready to meet us. We have learned that when Myla is ready, it's best to get out of her way and just let her fly.

While I finished getting dressed, I suddenly went from feeling uneasy to experiencing major contractions. They were quick and fierce. We took Ella to my sister's house, and on the way, I sat in the back of our gray Toyota Camry as we traversed Tampa, hitting what felt like every. Single. Bump. I spotted a semi behind us. He didn't stay far behind and seemed to follow us as we crossed the bridge into St. Pete. He must've been terrified by what he saw. Perhaps he was protecting other drivers from seeing me, because I was facing the trunk of the car, holding onto one, sometimes two, of those "Oh! Crap!" handles that most of us use to hang up dry cleaning. Jesus, heal him.

My poor husband could do nothing but drive. My contractions were three minutes apart as he zoomed into the drop-off zone at the birthing center. I could barely walk, stand, or sit. They ran the water to the bath, and while it was running, I got into the tub in immense pain. I breathed in and out. All I could do was focus on my breathing and one particular sign, which was perfectly positioned. In all caps, it read, *"Never, ever, ever, give up."* With that, I pushed three times, and out she flew. Had we hit any traffic along the way, she would've been born in the car.

I birthed an eight-and-a-half-pound girl, Myla Joy, without any medical intervention, laboring almost entirely in a moving car with a semi riding my tail. After that, something clicked, and I knew I could do anything.

For the next couple of years, I kept hearing the Lord talk to me about writing. In the midst of loud and precious voices of babies and toddlers, Jesus's voice isn't always the easiest to hear. He's patient. If you're in this stage, rest easy. Ask him lots of questions and take time with his answers. He makes accommodations for us. Just don't dismiss his voice as if he doesn't know you best. Take the small steps he's asking you to take and then keep waiting for him to unfold the rest. Making even moderate movement without him will frustrate you and everyone around you. That even applies when you're attempting to grow your family and the timing isn't right.

**We agreed on a home birth. Please don't be totally disgusted. It's really not a big deal.**

My sweet Cecelia Sunshine has a story all her own. When Myla was three, we really felt like our family wasn't complete. We tried for a year to get pregnant, to no avail. Frustrated, we concluded that perhaps the Lord wanted us to foster or adopt or both. We knew our hearts were ready for another child, but we didn't know where that child would come from. We filled out applications to our local fostering ministry. Excited and hopeful, we waited for our first class to commence. We spoke to our extended family. We explained our decision to Ella and Myla. We had prayed through the risks and concerns, and we felt peace with the direction we were headed.

One Saturday morning, just two days before our first foster classes, Mickey had a feeling I was pregnant. Husbands know these things. Sure enough, I took a test, which confirmed his suspicions. We were shocked and filled with joy and thanksgiving. For two days, I prayed about fostering. I wasn't sure what it would look like to bring in another child to our home while I was newly pregnant. I prayed that Jesus would help me walk with wisdom as we welcomed children into our home. I was nervous that I would fall short or be too tired to care for more children while I was pregnant. I shared it all with him.

On Monday, I had to call to tell the ministry our exciting news and to update them on my condition. The director told me that organization policy was to not allow pregnant women to begin the process of fostering. They wanted us to focus on the family God had provided. They said they would welcome us back when we were ready. The Lord shut a door I wouldn't have had the courage to close on my own. Guys, he's so good to us.

As we prepared to welcome Cecelia into our family, we decided that rushing to the hospital or a birthing center wouldn't be wise since she was the third and the second had come so quickly. We agreed on a home birth. Please don't be totally disgusted. It's really not a big deal. For the best and most hilarious education on home birth, let me direct you to the book *Dad is Fat* by Jim Gaffigan, a comedian with a slew of kids who's experienced a few home births with his wife. He says it all better than I ever could. My favorite line is "Homebirth? Why didn't you have the baby in that germ-infested building where sick people congregate? Didn't your wife want to give birth in a gown someone died in yesterday?"[13] That pretty much sums up our reasons right there. For us, homebirth was a wonderful experience. As long as I was afforded a healthy pregnancy, I would choose homebirth every time. Such a weirdo.

My labor started at midnight. The midwife rushed over to the house. We were all thinking that the birth would go quickly since the last one did. How wrong we were! My sweet Cecelia's head got stuck. Oh, man. Y'all, I was fully dilated and pushing for sixteen hours. It was awful.

I was exhausted. My husband was exhausted. We hadn't slept in thirty-six hours. I was an emotional wreck and couldn't concentrate. I shed many tears in pain and frustration. I didn't care how, I just wanted this to be over. I wanted to meet her. I wanted to rest.

It took an act of God, but finally her head released. All my effort was not in vain! I would meet her and soon! I didn't even have time to catch my breath between contractions. She was flying outta there like she was at Walmart trying to buy a TV on Black Friday. There was no stopping her. Except my midwife. She calmly and firmly instructed me: "Erin, you're not ready. Do not push. Hold here for a second."

Um . . . I'm sorry, what now?

So here's the thing, when a baby is at this late stage of birth, there is really no way to stop her from moving out of her current home. My body was physically ready to do what I wasn't supposed to do yet. I mean, I did my best to hold her in, but my body was screaming other ideas. My birthing team tried to help too. It was the worst pain I have ever felt, and I'm not a wuss about pain. But by this time, I had been in labor for so long and working so hard. The pain and the pressure had already lasted for sixteen solid hours! So when this last and most intense level of pain hit, well, I thought I was going to die. I can laugh now, knowing I didn't really die. But seriously, I had a moment when all I could think was "I won't meet my baby, but I'll be with Jesus." Yes, it was *that* physically painful and *that* physically difficult. Since I had never experienced that intensity level of pain before, I wasn't sure how much more I could handle. But God knew. And in one more push, she arrived. My Cecelia Sunshine, just one ounce shy of ten pounds.

Each time the Lord has conceived a desire in your heart, a purpose for you here on earth, it has to grow. It has to be birthed. You certainly have the option to abort those aspirations. You can kill the dreams he has for you. You can certainly make that choice. But his desire is for you to birth them, as painful and labor-intensive as that might be.

*Never, ever, ever give up.*

I wish I could tell you that for those sixteen hours of labor, I had these incredibly spiritual moments. But I didn't. I prayed once, around hour six, I think. It entailed a quick thanks to the Lord for giving me the baby we had prayed for so desperately. Then I asked him to help me get her out quickly. It was that simple. I didn't need to say much more because I knew he was there the whole time. I knew he was the giver of my life and this new little life inside me. He is the author of my story and yours. I knew he had a plan for both of us. I trusted him. And when everything was at its worst—the most painful and exhausting—my hope was still Jesus. Meeting him was my worst-case scenario. What a great option!

The things I've birthed in my life spiritually take shape in similar ways to the ways in which my girls have grown outside the womb. They take time to mature. When we are given the opportunity to see our dreams come to maturity, our faith is strengthened, and our hope is renewed. The process, although painfully, tediously slow at times, is worth it. The funny thing is, it's only slow to us. God lives outside time. For him, it's on schedule. He's not in a hurry to get anywhere. He just wants to be with us. Just like the birthing of children, his original design in this process is to bring the parents closer to each other and closer to him. What he is asking you to birth is intended to bring you closer to him. Whatever happens with the thing itself is a bonus.

This bears repeating. I have never felt more fully aligned with Jesus than I have in birthing this book or birthing my children. Jesus wants us to leave the details and the release of what we birth to him. Which is why, in each decision we've made with our children—from their names, to their births, to their schooling, to their device usage—we pray. I do not know what I am doing. I know that I don't. The moment I believe that *I* have the power to raise them into wonderful, contributing, generous, passionate daughters of God is the moment I have stopped asking him what he says about them. Pride has found its way into my heart when I think I know my kids better than he does.

In fact, I feel so inadequate dedicating part of this book to raising them that I tucked it right here toward the end. I don't have a whole lot to share here because we have no way of knowing if what we're doing is working. So, I will repeat: my big secret in raising these amazing girls is to talk to Jesus about them. That's it. I talk with God and let his wisdom reign. Sometimes this drives my kids crazy. Like we're always living on the edge. We are. It's called the edge of grace. We fall off the mountain of our own ideas constantly. Praise Jesus.

My three, make-me-lose-my-breath, beautiful girls have asked my husband and me many, many times for a list of rules. This turns my soul into knots. The idea of rules taped up somewhere in their rooms or my home is terrifying and reeks of perfectionism. Given my past, I know that I don't want to raise, good, rule-following daughters. I want passionate, sold-out, lovers of the heart of God. The former will come as fruit of the latter. So instead of reading all the books on parenting, we spend time with them, we pray, read the Word,

**Like we're always living on the edge. We are. It's called the edge of grace. We fall off the mountain of our own ideas constantly. Praise Jesus.**

and instruct. We live the way we want them to live: running after Jesus, clinging to him, worshipping him, working out what he says, taking risks with him, with joy and fear and trembling. We rely fully on the promises of God and what we find in his Word: forgiveness, grace, mercy, self-control, gentleness, respect, and compassion. We practice those things, too, by his power and strength.

The boundaries we create for each child are different because each one is so different. The prayers for each girl are different too. And yes, all this is a slow payoff, like a retirement account. You pay in, pay in, pay in, to this savings of sorts, which has value on its own. But like a retirement account, we have faith in the law of compounding interest, making deposits early and often, trusting that over time, the deposits will yield a high return, exceedingly more than we could've ever seen on our own. With our girls, we trust God's law of love; we know it yields the highest return. And it turns out, because of my past, I've become pretty skeptical of a quick payoff anyway.

I pray for and about everything. I even go so far as to pray that I pray the right prayers for them. I pray that God would uncover the mysteries of who my daughters are. I pray that they would know how much we love and pray for them. I pray they would always know how much we rely on the Lord to be the parents we are to them. I pray we would be wise in leaving them a spiritual and financial legacy of love and generosity. I pray they would experience the joy of following Christ and the inheritance of freedom that he bought for them. I pray they would know when to be silent and when to speak up. I pray kindness and truth would mark their decisions. I pray for their safety; I pray for their purpose. Of course, I pray that they would be shielded from the influence of the world. I intercede, like my mama and daddy did for me.

Guess where some of this praying led to. Homeschooling. Sigh. I had no idea what I was getting myself into. I could write another book about this choice, but it would be far more whiney and much more vulnerable. I'm still in the thick of it. I have more questions than answers. I'm beginning to see the fruit of our prayers and decisions, but they're still blossoming.

Let me answer your plaguing questions and assumptions before I move on:

❑ I am not more patient than you are.

❑ I don't think homeschooling is for every person.

❑ It was never my plan to homeschool.

❑ We don't do school in our pj's. I have strong opinions about this for myself and my family.

❑ I don't know how long I'll homeschool.

And yes, my kids are weird. I love us, but we're weird.

The truth is, I don't want normal kids. I am not normal. The ways of God are not normal. I am proud of that. If homeschooling has anything to do with it, then I'm happy to partner with the Lord on this adventure. I will only do it as he calls me to it. I ask him every year because truly I couldn't do it if it wasn't a part of his will for our family. Bye to all three of my Felicias. No thanks.

Literally, every year of the six years I've homeschooled, the school year starts, and I say, "I'm not ready."

The back-to-school posts start filling up my social media feed. With every scroll, I see adorable children holding chalkboard signs announcing their grade and their favorites and sporting new shoes and slicked-back hair. I see mamas posing proudly with their kiddos. And then, as I sit there examining the perfectly wrinkle-free faces with every hair in place at 7 a.m., a wave of fear and regret grips my heart. I'm immobilized because I'm only two sips into my coffee and still in my pajamas, but in my heart, I'm half-way down the street chasing the school bus, screaming, "Waaaaaaaaaaaaaaait! I'm not ready for this!"

Yep, the first day of school marks the moment each year when I push the doubts I dare not admit to the corners of my mind. I don't want to homeschool my kids.

It's year six of homeschooling. I don't think a single year has started with me thinking: This is going to be so awesome! I'm so excited to be doing this! I really want to homeschool my kids. Nope. And I'm an unabashedly optimistic person. This year has been no different.

I know a lot of diehard homeschool families and mamas. But I am not one of them. I envy their planning boards and blogs; the rhythm of their day astounds me. We are all clunks and bangs over here. We haven't found our stride yet. I'm beginning to wonder if there *is* such a thing.

So why do I homeschool my children?

**Here is my go-to answer:**

It works well for our family.

Full disclosure: Most days, this is true. We own a business, and occasionally my husband works nights and weekends. Since we homeschool, he can arrange his schedule to hang out with us in the morning if he has to work in the evening. In the morning, this is like a dream come true, and we are the poster family for homeschooling. By evening, we are suffering from the consequences of our upside-down schedule. Inevitably, the children or I or both will be in tears somewhere around 8 p.m., trying to finish a math lesson. By the time my husband gets home, I am looking up late enrollment options for local schools.

Let me assure you. It doesn't *always* work well.

**Here is my follow-up answer:**

Homeschooling takes us half the amount of time of a normal school day, which gives us more time to explore other interests.

Full disclosure: Make no mistake; half-time lessons are essential to our ability to homeschool. We can squeeze in a lesson while we wait in the pediatrician's office; they can bring books with them while I'm running

141

errands; or we can go on a field trip in the morning with friends and still have time for school work in the afternoon. But sometimes that extra half-day destroys nearly every room in my house. Those four hours breed our friends named mischief and mayhem, and they run scandalously through shelves of neatly held books and painstakingly built Lego towns. Those extra few hours feed imagination and creativity in my children's minds to the point that I am "not allowed to go into any bedroom in the house because all the babies at the daycare are sleeping." Which begs the question, "Is the daycare 'director' allowed to sneak in there and take a nap, too, because *you tiny people are exhausting, and I am absolutely going into my own bedroom. Move it.*"

With our extra time, we often explore the interesting world of forgiveness.

Truthfully, my family and I wax and wane between taking an indefinite leave of absence and really loving our days of home education. How do we decide—how do any of us really decide—what's the right thing for our kids, for us, for our family? We ask the One who loved our families before we were even born, who loves you and me. The problem is, we don't always like the way he answers, which brings me to the God-honest reason for heading down this homeschool path:

We believe this is God's best for our family. We believe he called us to it. I was really trying to hear something—anything—else. Letting go of my own plans was heartbreaking. Then a friend shared this passage in Romans 12:1–2 with me.

> So here's what I want you to do, God helping you: Take your everyday, ordinary life—your sleeping, eating, going-to-work, and walking-around life—and place it before God as an offering. Embracing what God does for you is the best thing you can do for him. Don't become so well-adjusted to your culture that you fit into it without even thinking. Instead, fix your attention on God. You'll be changed from the inside out. Readily recognize what he

wants from you, and quickly respond to it. Unlike the culture around you, always dragging you down to its level of immaturity, God brings the best out of you, develops well-formed maturity in you (MSG).

So that's what we did. We offered our lives to the Lord and (eventually) embraced what he wanted us to do.

This willful obedience to his plan for my life is where I have experienced the most triumphant victories and the most humbling defeats. In this homeschooling place, I have to fix my attention on him. I absolutely cannot do this without him. Day in and day out, this journey draws me nearer to the throne where I once again lay down the reigns of control.

And my tiny people, they see it all. They see me wrestle with concerns that come from this every-day, ordinary life. Eventually they see me lay those down too. They see me change here. That's the purpose of it. That's why he asked me to do this. He orchestrated this because he loves me, and whatever develops in my kids during this journey is the fruit of the work he's doing in me. When I love his plan, I love it because I see the fruit. It's hard to love something when it's taking shape. Yet this is where I experience God's maturity forming in me, albeit slowly.

Thankfully, this very real place keeps me standing—I should probably be kneeling—in humility and for the most part, out of the judgment seat. Lord knows, next school year, or tomorrow, I'll need you to be judgment-free if you see me chasing the school bus in tears.

**Daughters and Sons**

Last year, I was at an orientation for one of my kid's co-op classes with over one hundred mamas in the room. Most of these moms are extremely accomplished. They are: going to school themselves while homeschooling their children, fostering sibling sets, working full-time jobs, leading ministries, and/or working toward their bachelors, masters, or doctorate degrees. These parents include former public school teachers, parents who have already raised several children, world travelers, and more. Scanning the room, I was beginning to feel excited again about our enrollment in the program. Across the room, I spotted a friend I had grown up with who was now a pastor and father of five. He was easy to spot, since he was the only man in a sea of women. He was there in place of his wife who normally took on the role of lead teacher in their homeschooling endeavor. We were catching up while our kids were holding up a wall, lost in the world of Minecraft, when the director of the program came up to us. She said to my friend, "Well, it looks like you're the only male here, so I'll need you to open us up in prayer."

You should know that I am ill-equipped to hide my facial expressions, including disgust. I can't hide my emotions of annoyance or revulsion when faced with injustice. I had all three that day. He wasn't chosen to pray at that moment because he's a pastor. In a room full of accomplished women, all undoubtedly able to handle the rigors of *raising* men, all of us were overlooked. We weren't considered equipped enough to pray for women, children, and one solitary man. It occurred to me that day that my work is here too. My work is to my children and to the people in my community, no matter their beliefs. My hope is that I will pour out to those around from the living water within me that Jesus spoke about to the Samaritan woman in John 4.

Everywhere I go, I have been called to bring freedom. So have you. Even— and sometimes especially—in our Christian circles. But it's difficult, isn't it? I see great joy in leading people to the throne of grace for the very first time. I also know a major portion of my calling is to encourage and teach the church. Paul told us not to neglect one over the other. In fact, he said whatever you do for the lost, be sure to do for the church in even greater measure.

So then, whatever I do for the unreached, I must do in greater measure for my own church family, and whatever I do for my own church family, I must do in even greater measure still for my family at home. Does this already make you feel tired and overwhelmed? I don't mean for it to. I think for far too long, we've been trying to do all the things, spin all the tops, hold all the plates, and balance all the books. But we can't. We weren't made to.

Just like at the water park, this is what our churches should look like, just letting it spill out. Instead, we don't know how to reconcile the temptation of this world with the righteousness of God. So we think our way out—just like my kids—is through a list of rules. Rules aren't the heart of God. Relationship is.

Let me give you an example of this. Many churches historically and even today invoke modesty standards and dress codes for men and women, but most of these aren't on display; they are simply understood, rooted in tradition. On my visits to other churches, I've even seen these rules posted. It's shocking to stare at these types of messages and rules, rules I'm certain are birthed out of a righteous desire to protect the congregation from temptation. But rules don't help that way. If they did, we'd still be under Levitical law. God knows—and we should be reminded—rules don't create changes in the heart, grace does. Law leads us to grace because without grace, we would be slaves to the law.

Recently, I started to see some unsettling trends seeping out of the church. My prayers enlarged from praying off the oppression and temptations of this world to addressing the oppression of women I saw lingering within the family of God. And remember, we have to get it right here first. I don't think I ever saw it growing up or before I had kids. But once I began raising girls, I realized that it's there.

I've been fortunate to land in a church that elevates women. There is no glass ceiling. They ask what God is saying without questioning to whom he might be saying it. I love that. I have a place to use my gifts. Gifts my Creator specifically knit into me, not into my husband. My husband has a place to use his gifts. Gifts his Creator specifically knit into him, not into me. There is a place for both of us. We are not the same, but we are equal.

So what do these rules do? They perpetuate a belief that both a woman and a man's identity are rooted in who we are as sexual beings. You can imagine because of my past that I was once chained to and am now freed from, this, to me, is unacceptable.

This is how the *world* identifies us. When we bring these ideas into the church and view women and their bodies as forms of seduction and as the devil's playground, we rob women and men of seeing each other in our truest design: spirit, soul, and body. In that order.

I am a spirit; I have a soul; I live in a body.

When we neglect to see each other in the glorious light of the first two, then the problem is not with, in this case, the woman who lives in the body. The problem is with the man's lack of spiritual truth, ignorance in his own mind, and slavery to his own body.

Seeing these rules listed in a church rocked me. We are missing it. This is a grave offense toward women to put the curves of their hips and chest under scrutiny. These rules don't benefit women. These rules justify men whose bodies have become their masters. If you see women as temptresses, then their clothing won't change your view of them. What shall we do as women so that we are seen as spirits with intelligence, personalities, and emotions who have been given womanly bodies, made in the image and likeness of God? Should we cut off the parts that don't look like Jesus when he walked as a human on earth? Would that make us more holy?

This twisted perception doesn't just affect women but affects men as well.

When we were in Haiti, one young man was moved by the affection he could freely show in a country not his own. I hadn't even considered this at the time, but I can see it so clearly now. He loves kids. As a young man, he works at camps and desires to pour into the young men of his community.

But in the United States, he worries that his expressive nature might be misinterpreted. He shared with us how difficult it is to play and be affectionate with kids because of the fear of being misunderstood. And he's right. How many of us feel uncomfortable when we see a

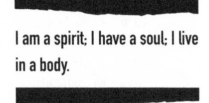

**I am a spirit; I have a soul; I live in a body.**

child sitting on a man's lap who is not his or her father? A small percentage of sexual deviants have perverted a beautiful and godly representation of innocent comradery and discipling. In Haiti, those kids were desperate for tenderness and human contact, and so was my friend.

We have to talk about these tough subjects in the church. We have to see things clearly as the family of God to protect and educate one another. We can't be afraid to have these very difficult conversations. These are the questions plaguing this generation of youth around the world and the questions of the #metoo and the feminist movement that blow up my social media news feed. Frankly, on some occasions, these questions are better answered by non-believers than by preachers. Non-answers to these questions, resistance to the truth, and the current mandates of the church when it comes to these issues are unacceptable for me, my husband and for our three girls. They are equally unacceptable for boys who are being raised in the church. It is an abuse of power to not correct this for the sake of every man that holds a position or who has been given the blessing of authority in the church. You must find truth. You must ask yourself if we are first looking at one another the way God sees us through Jesus's blood as a pure and undefiled spirit with a unique soul. Then perhaps we will no longer see each other as shamefully naked as Adam and Eve did in light of their own sin, needing to hide.

## FOR THE DAUGHTERS OF GOD:

My own daughters, my nieces, my sisters, the young women we mentor, and the friends of my daughters, please hear me. You are far more than the gender God has blessed you with. You are more than a temptation for men. Do you hear that? You are more than your beautiful hair, your long fingernails, your frame, your curves, your most blessed parts. You have strength in your character, conviction in your heart, passion in your bones, compassion in your eyes, and joy in your smile. You are servants: pastors, prophets, apostles, evangelists, and teachers. You are warriors for justice with an intellect that seeks first to understand. I see you, young woman of God. You are more than how you dress, how short your hair is, how much make up you wear, the gap in your thighs, the plumpness of your lips, or the number on a scale. You are entirely beautiful and acceptable. In fact, your beauty stands alone. Try as you might to compare it to others around you, you can't. You, beloved, are incomparable.

## YOU BELONG HERE.

While you are here on this earth, I pray you know that it is a blessing and honor to be a woman. If the Lord gives you children through your womb, it is a beautiful journey. Don't mock it or minimize it. Be considerate of those who choose not to or aren't able to bear children. God's purposes for us are far greater than we can assume.

If he enables you to be a mother through birth, adoption, fostering, or discipleship, I pray you find the utmost joy in the nurturing aspects of your mothering, wherever and however it shows up. It is a place

I've never felt more alive. I pray nurturing relationships, sharing emotions, and showing kindness are no longer misrepresented as a woman's characteristics, but they would be celebrated as godly. Don't let those qualities in you ever be diminished. Protect the beauty of them within you.

If the Lord allows you to be married to a man to whom you commit your body and life, honor him with it. Don't use it for manipulation or selfish gain. Truly love your husband with all of you, for love is not self-seeking. Don't wait for the other person to stop being selfish. That in itself is self-seeking. Mutually submit to each other. Speak truth over him and loving truth about him. And girl, pray for him. You will both need it.

Love and live the same way in your friendships. Fight and sacrifice for deep relationships. Encourage your tribe. Protect them and what God's blessed you with. Allow them to do the same for you. If they choose not to love you in the same way, guard your heart and keep your distance until they are worthy of your trust. I pray they would become better because of your influence. Don't give up on them. Pray them back.

I pray your confidence comes from the Lord in who he made you to be. He will guide you in your career choice, your education, your creative pursuits, when to bravely speak, when to listen, when to fight, and when to yield. If you listen, he will tell you who you are. He will tell you when you forget, as we all do, through his Word and by way of the still, small voice of the Holy Spirit. Learn to listen to and trust that voice. The other voices of this world will try to be louder and bolder and might even sound like truth, but his is the one that matters. Line it up against every other voice. Even mine. For I have even been wrong about what God was doing in you.

## FOR THE SONS OF GOD:

My nephews, my brothers, the young men we mentor, and the friends of my daughters, please hear me. You are more than ogling idiots at the mercy of your fleshly desires. You are far more than the world would want us to believe about you. You are not easily seduced by this world because you are grounded in faith. You are more than merciless, mindless fools without conviction in your heart, without a love for those around you. Your heart is more than lust and passion. It angers me that the world feeds that lie to us and to you. You are more than video-gamers, escaping from this world to live in a fantasy you can control. I know it. I have seen your gentleness, your kindness, your affection toward the young and old, the weak and strong.

## YOU ARE NEEDED HERE.

You are more than the sum of your parts. You are more than strong arms and fast feet. You are more than a booming voice and a powerful handshake. You are servants: pastors, prophets, apostles, evangelists, and teachers. You are creative; you are well-read and filled with joy and conviction. You dance, sing, worship, and rejoice like King David. There is power in the way you help and guide and profound strength in your emotion. You are protectors of the innocent and champions of change. You link arms with your sisters, shedding the same tears, listening with intention, and longing for the identical change we do, hopeful that, as far as it concerns you, change will come. How brave you are.

If the Lord wills it, you might be husbands or daddies one day. When you are, let gentleness and mercy guide you. Your strength attracts the attention of this world, but your tenderness is like a wrecking ball to the hardest heart. Lead from there. It heals; it invites; it changes things.

I am so thankful for you.

For neither men nor women were meant to walk these pilgrim days without the other. We are meant to pioneer together, which is impossible if one gender doesn't belong. So you have waited, you have said, I will not go where there is no room for my sister, especially in the name of Jesus. I see you, bro. I thank you. You honor me, my husband, and our daughters. You look like the Jesus I know and tell them about. May the Lord repay your resolve to see change. In our lifetime, may we see the church rising up together, saying in unity: we are different, but you are my equal. We need each other, and we need Jesus to fill in our gaps.

I pray all this for us, in the name of Jesus. Amen.

## LET'S REFLECT:

Think about the analogy of the water park at the beginning of the chapter. How have you tried to balance rules and temptation when you've been created to overflow with love?

Is there something in your life that you feel like God is birthing? Where are you in that process: is it still being formed, are you in transition, is it a newborn baby, or is it maturing?

How would you view women and men differently if you chose to see them the way Jesus does: as spiritual beings first?

How would the church look different if men and women formed a unified front against the enemy of truth?

YOU'RE RAISING UP A WARRIOR,

FROM MY TIMID PRAYER.

I WON'T FEAR THE BATTLE

FOR YOU ARE WITH ME THERE.

**"YOU OVERWHELM ME"**

**VALLEY'S END**

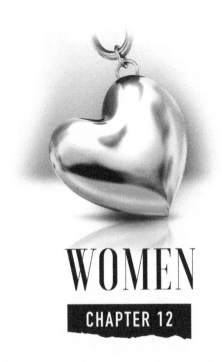

# WOMEN

## CHAPTER 12

I spend most mornings watching the sunrise with Jesus. I wasn't always a morning person. I still don't think I am. But I'm a Jesus person. The early morning hour(s) before my kids rise with all their clamoring and questions gives me the perfect quiet space to listen, receive, and meditate on the beauty of my Savior. I sip my coffee—Must. Have. Coffee—pour out my heart, ask questions, pray, sing songs, get on my knees, or do some combination. This quiet space with a stunning sunrise as a backdrop weaves heaven into my day. It readies me for the earthly kingdom I will inevitably face. It is a gift every time I rise.

On the mornings when I am not quick to get up, I often envision him pulling out the chair for me at our kitchen table, inviting me to talk with him again. He says some version of, "I've got so much to tell you." And that's about all it takes. I'm up and out of my alluring bed because I can't wait to hear everything my Lord, my Teacher, my Friend, my Love has to say. Sometimes in my eagerness, I do all the talking and don't let him speak. Why do I do that? What he says is a treasure of wealth and oh-so-deep. And all my wandering thoughts seem empty. He listens anyway, and somehow even that's more than what I need.

In these moments, he renews my mind about who I am and what he's called me to be. He refines me and guides me. He leads me to a greater understanding of my identity and purpose. Here he pours into me that I might pour into others. Here, in these quiet morning moments, he first led me to step up to leadership in our church. This is where he first led me to write, first led me to quit a job I thought I loved, and he first prompted me to speak from the pulpit.

This is where he first prompted me to teach his Word outside my familiar weekly women's Bible study. The pull tugged so strongly at my heart in those early hours. God was urging me to go to church that day and tell our teaching pastor that I was ready to teach. Yep, you read that right.

I had some serious doubts about God's direction. I shared them all with the Lord. Our conversation went a little like this.

Me: Ummmm . . . I'm not ready to teach. Teach what? Also, I don't think I should tell him. Maybe asking would be better. But that's beside the point. I just don't want to. Why? Why should I? No. I can't. No.

My Father: Erin, if you were encouraging someone else in this situation to step out in faith, what would you say to them?

Me: I know where this is going. No. Please, Lord, you can't really be asking me to do this. Aaaaggghhhhhhh!

My Father: Yes, I am asking you. Now if it were a sister or brother who didn't think they were qualified for what I was asking them to do, I am certain I would prompt you to remind them: If God is for you, who can be against you? You cannot fail. What can mere mortals do to you? He's given you everything you need for life and godliness.

Me (Sigh): I know you're right. You've said this to me a thousand times.

And then he led me to this passage in Luke 10:21–24.

> At that same time Jesus was filled with the joy of the Holy Spirit, and he said, "O Father, Lord of heaven and earth, thank you for hiding these things from those who think themselves wise and clever, and for revealing them to the childlike. Yes, Father, it pleased you to do it this way. "My Father has entrusted everything to me. No one truly knows the Son except the Father, and no one truly knows the Father except the Son and those to whom the Son chooses to reveal him." Then when they were alone, he turned to the disciples and said, "Blessed are the eyes that see what you have seen. I tell you, many prophets and kings longed to see what you see, but they didn't see it. And they longed to hear what you hear, but they didn't hear it" (NLT).

My Father: I choose *you* to reveal my truth. It's for you first, my chosen daughter. Now it's time to share it.

Me (sighing heavily again): I guess. Okay.

I'm sure if God wasn't the kind of loving Father he is, then he would've rolled his eyes at me. Even as I write this, I want to throat-punch myself for my unbelief. Ugh. Thank God for his gentleness and patience with us. Amiright?

After this difficult conversation, we made our way to church. Our pastor finished up worship and started flipping through his Bible as he stepped up to the pulpit.

He said, "Before I begin with my message, I just needed to share this word I received during worship. Bear with me while I find it. Ah, here it is. Luke 10."

Full stop. What?!

You guys, my jaw dropped. From the first word, I absolutely could not stop sobbing. I knew what I had to do. I had to share what God was asking of me. I had to step out. I had to tell him I was ready to teach.

I wrestled with my decision, doubting through the rest of that message. I hadn't even told my husband what the Lord had been unraveling in me during the last couple of hours. I wanted to ask him if I was being foolish or if I should step out. I wanted his approval and his encouragement. I was stalling.

In the midst of my tears, the Lord stopped me and gave me this verse:

Galatians 4:6–7 tells us, "And because we are his children, God has sent the Spirit of his Son into our hearts, prompting us to call out, 'Abba, Father.' Now you are no longer a slave but God's own child. And since you are his child, God has made you his heir" (NLT).

Then he sealed these words on my heart in a way I could never explain: "You are my daughter. Let my spirit remind you as it cries out from within you that you are an heir to my kingdom. All I have is yours. I have qualified you. You have heard from me. What more do you need?"

So. much. crying.

I finally surrendered. "You're right, Father. I hear you calling my name. I will tell our pastor and leave the rest up to you."

I was received fully by the leadership at our church, which I know doesn't come so easily for many women. I had my first opportunity to speak during the Sunday night service just a few weeks later. But the first time I preached in front of my entire congregation on a Sunday morning was on a Mother's Day. I had invited several women whom I admire. One was our dear babysitter and friend. She couldn't make it because she needed to be at her church with her mama. But when I saw her a few days later, she exasperatedly said, "I wish I would've come to hear you speak. The title of the message at *my* church on Mother's Day was, 'The Weaker Vessel.'"

Oh, my Lord.

Though I don't think about it often, in times like these, it occurs to me that some men and women do not think that God wants women to ever teach men in any context within the kingdom of God. I think this is as good as place as any to address that.

**The scandal of Jesus's grace is that it is available to everyone in the same measure. When we have come to the throne of grace, how can we stay silent?**

The Bible is filled with women who contributed to the preaching of the gospel by their own means and with their own voices. The scandal of Jesus's grace is that it is available to everyone in the same measure. When we have come to the throne of grace, how can we stay silent? When freedom has been offered to us, how can we keep it to ourselves? The nature of God is to share, to give. Moses shows us that. He was reluctant to speak, but he did it anyway—in spite of a serious speech impediment, a stutter that hindered him even further. He struggled with God too. But when all was said and done, he obeyed. He proclaimed freedom to the captive Israelites. When Pharaoh wouldn't release the people of Israel to be free in their chosen-ness, God sent famine and plagues to the region. These broke down Pharaoh's resolve until finally, in the anguish of his sorrow, fear, and grief, he released the Israelites.

Exodus 12:31 says, "Pharaoh sent for Moses and Aaron during the night. 'Get out!' he ordered. 'Leave my people—and take the rest of the Israelites with you! Go and worship the LORD as you have requested'" (NLT).

Just like Pharaoh, some leaders of our churches can try to contain our chosen-ness. While that's not okay, it need not confine you. Friend, regardless of your gender, you are free to go and worship the Lord as you have requested, which I hope is free from the confines of gender inequality. If you keep your eyes fixed on what God knows about you, then what he does next for you will be just like what he did for the Israelites. He will show his favor and love toward you. His glory will be on display. Freedom will be released.

This is the truest picture of the church. When we are seeking the heart of God, then we respond to the cry of one oppressed heart. Sometimes we are on the physical frontlines of the battle: clothing, feeding, and ministering to the very real needs of God's people. Sometimes we are on the frontlines of the spiritual war, praying for things in the spirit that we cannot see in the natural. Sometimes we're somewhere in between. When we do this together, we experience Jesus's peace, power, love, fruit, gifts, and favor. This occurs when we act in faith and surrender—a surrender that expects freedom to be released.

What we see most often from Jesus is a release of women into freedom from their sexual misdeeds or gender role constraints: the adulteress; the woman at the well; the woman with the issue of blood; Mary Magdalene; Martha; Mary of Bethany, Mary, the mother of Jesus; Elizabeth, the mother of John the Baptist; Claudia, the wife of Pontius Pilate; and others. To all these women, Jesus expressed freedom. In essence, saying: You are more than a sexual being to me. I am going to free you. You are an essential and useful member of my kingdom, not because of how your body performs but because of what your spirit and soul holds.

Sometimes we miss this. We see Jesus performing these miracles of freedom for women, and we have wrongly associated women's sin with their sexuality or their gender roles. Instead, we can take from this what Jesus truly meant to show us through these women: that they and we are more than sexual beings, used for sex, punished for sex, and/or temptresses of sex.

Neither did Jesus allow us to be subject to culturally imposed gender roles. He tore down all those barriers and stereotypes with the veil. May we agree with Jesus. May we work like he did for the release of oppression for women and men. While Jesus clearly advocated for the freedom of women, Paul's words are often used to justify the silencing of women in church. Let's go directly to the verse that is so often quoted and interpreted with prejudice, shall we?

"Therefore, *I* encourage the men to pray on every occasion with hands lifted to God in worship with clean hearts, free from frustration or strife. And that the women would also pray with clean hearts, dressed appropriately and adorned modestly and sensibly, not flaunting their wealth. But they should be recognized instead by their beautiful deeds of kindness, suitable as one who worships God. Let the women who are new converts be willing to learn with all submission to their leaders and not speak out of turn. *I* don't advocate that the newly converted women be the teachers in the church, assuming authority over the men, but to live in peace" (1 Timothy 2:8–12, TPT, emphasis added).

"*I* desire therefore that the men pray everywhere, lifting up holy hands, without wrath and doubting; in like manner also, that the women adorn themselves in modest apparel, with propriety and moderation, not with braided hair or gold or pearls or costly clothing, but, which is proper for women professing godliness, with good works. Let a woman learn in silence with all submission. And *I* do not permit a woman to teach or to have authority over a man, but to be in silence" (1 Timothy 2:8–12, NKJV, emphasis added).

"In every place of worship, *I* want men to pray with holy hands lifted up to God, free from anger and controversy. And I want women to be modest in their appearance. They should wear decent and appropriate clothing and not draw attention to themselves by the way they fix their hair or by wearing gold or pearls or expensive clothes. For women who claim to be devoted to God should make themselves attractive by the good things they do. Women should learn quietly and submissively. *I* do not let women teach men or have authority over them. Let them listen quietly" (1 Timothy 2:8–12, NLT, emphasis added).

There it is. There it is. There it is.

Now, come, let us reason together because God gave us the ability to think and explain, to research and study. When we become Christians, we don't leave our minds at the gate where we entered into the kingdom of God. We get to bring our intellect with us, hallelujah! So let's not waste it. Shall we discard the miracles he performed, the very scandalous grace he doled out to women and men because of one isolated passage from Paul's instructions? Should we build a whole theology out of one section of Scripture? Or should we ask better questions about what he meant?

Now I agree that there is a time for men and women both to be silent. When Elizabeth became pregnant with John the Baptist, her husband, Zechariah was so suspect of the whole miracle that the Lord silenced him for the duration of her pregnancy. It would seem that if we were to take Paul's letter to Timothy literally for every church for all time, then perhaps we should show the same honor to the silencing of preachers when they are slow to agree with a miracle. Of course, this argument is ridiculous. Yet that's exactly what has happened in the letter to Timothy. People—albeit well-intentioned—have taken this passage and twisted it out of context.

Let's give some context to this story Paul is writing to Timothy at Ephesus. In the middle of Ephesus was the temple of Artemis, one of the Seven Wonders of the Ancient World. This temple was a massive structure four times as large as the Athenian Parthenon and featuring 127 columns stretching sixty feet high.[14] The temple itself was a wonder, and many came from all around the region to worship here. Paul was extending encouragement and insight to Timothy because Paul was first a missionary to this area. He knew the trials facing Timothy and needed to direct him well.

The worshippers at this temple bowed to the goddess Artemis, the goddess of fertility. Because of this, their worship elevated women, especially fertile women, to god-like status. The women were revered and led most of the festivals and services. When Paul and Timothy came to preach the good news of Jesus, they had to overcome a different kind of gender inequality. The women who were used to talking and leading were just learning the truth for themselves. This was not a time for them to be teaching. This was a time for them to be students. That's what Paul is reminding Timothy of, in this specific letter, to this specific region.

There might be churches where the voices of men are oppressed. Where the gossip or complaints of women or men inhibit worship. We have to lead well, like Paul, and pay attention when there is a time for silence. Each church in the New Testament times had specific needs, just like our churches do today. Here Paul leaves a guiding principle for one specific church that faced a problem that might still exist in certain churches today. Let's just be sure this problem actually exists before we forever apply this verse to all women preachers.

In the story of Zechariah, we know that the angel of the Lord's desire was to silence him in his unbelief or to keep him from prideful boasting. That's a great time for silence. We ought to be silent when our faith is small or when we are struggling with ungratefulness. We need time to reflect and be reminded of the mighty God we serve. Otherwise what story of amazing grace do we have to share? How can we love well when our faith is small?

We have to understand the context for silence lest we oppress the necessary and diverse voices of our church. Jesus's desire was to elevate the voice and credibility of women. He knew there were times when the best way to do that was to be silent. Which is why, when Jesus stood before Pontius Pilate, the governor who sealed his fate on the cross, he spoke one line and then remained quiet.

> "Now Jesus stood before the governor. And the governor asked Him, saying, 'Are You the King of the Jews?' Jesus said to him, 'It is as you say'" (Matthew 27:11, NKJV).

In fact, he was more than the king of the Jews: he was the Messiah, righteous, and without fault. After Jesus responds to Pilate's questions, the chief priests and elders that were in the judge's hall started hurling accusations at Jesus, but to them, Jesus gave no reply. No defense. No response. He said *nada*.

In the face of horrendous accusations, though he was provoked, he remained wordless. In this one setting, in the Gospel of Matthew, Jesus didn't need to come to his own defense. He had no need to explain matters of the kingdom of heaven. What's fascinating is, while Jesus is being indicted by the governor of Judea, our Messiah, disinclined to speak for himself, allowed a woman to defend his righteousness.

**But to Jesus, she had a voice; she had a powerful message, and out of his deep love for her, he stayed silent so that her voice could be heard.**

Claudia, Pontius Pilate's own wife, was that woman. In the New Testament, she is nameless and is only mentioned in the Gospel of Matthew. Most scholars agree, however, that she is the Claudia mentioned in 2 Timothy as one of the faithful evangelists who worked to spread the message of Christ.[15]

To the men of the age, the big players in this scene were Pilate, Annas (Ananias), Caiaphas, Peter, Judas, and the other disciples, and rightly so. But then, right in the middle of this scene, we're introduced to a nameless woman barely worth mentioning. But to Jesus, she had a voice; she had a powerful message, and out of his deep love for her, he stayed silent so that her voice could be heard. The Truth (Jesus) was not silenced because *she*—a woman!—proclaimed his righteousness among men. She bore witness.

And in what is possibly the most ironic scene in the Bible, we see Jesus Christ, the Word of God, before the judge's seat. She was not even seen or permitted to enter the court. She wasn't considered a viable witness in Jerusalem during this period of time. But there she was anyway, a woman interrupting an emotional, tense, and chaotic moment in the most important trial ever. *Ever*!

She sends a message to her husband and says, "Have nothing to do with that *righteous and innocent Man*, for last night I suffered greatly in a dream because of Him" (Matthew 27:19, AMP, emphasis added).

We don't know what her dream was about. We don't know what she might have seen that made her suffer so greatly. I have ideas. I want to speculate. One day, I'll know, but it doesn't matter here. What matters is she was deeply moved in her spirit and she. Spoke. Up. What you'll see from Jesus most often in his interactions with women is how he inspires, requests, and even commands them to speak.

When she sent that message, she spoke powerfully against the establishment. She spoke up for innocence; she spoke up for freedom; she spoke up for her Savior. She spoke up despite her husband, the lawmakers, the judges, the teachers of the law, the highest officials, and the deeply religious. She spoke up to the most powerful men in all history. She spoke up to the men that would sentence the Son of God to death. This woman was the *only* person who spoke up on his behalf.

Comparatively, right after this, Peter, Jesus's closest friend, denied that he even knew Jesus.

When Claudia experienced the truth about who Jesus was, it came to her spirit by a dream or a vision. That experience stirred her so deeply that it shifted her loyalty from her government, her position, her ethnicity—and even her husband—to her Savior.

That is a scary place. Erin, are really asking me to shift my loyalty from my spouse?

My answer is that it never should be on man—any man—in the first place. How can this be biblical? Because no earthly man or woman can fill a place where the heavenly God belongs. The seat of your heart was made for Jesus, and he alone is worthy of that space. You are first a child of God. Your devotion lies first to him and what he is calling you to do.

Now because he is my Creator, my Savior, and my Redeemer, his love for me is generous. He will implore me to turn my heart back toward loving Mickey and the rest of his beloved children, and he will equip and empower me to do so with his love. It is so much easier to hide behind our spouses and gender roles rather than letting Christ redefine us. Your loyalty and obedience to Jesus is sacred and shouldn't be given flippantly. Go with grace on your journey of obedience and surrender.

As a woman, most of my decisions are usually based on my relationships and how they might be affected by said decision. As a little girl, I played with dolls or played house because I tended to view the world in relational terms. Let me shake things up for you: that is not God's design for just me because I'm a girl. His design is for both women *and* men to desire and need relationships with each other through him. The *sin* of Adam and Eve created the gender gap and roles that define our relationships and society today. The cross redeemed us from the chasm that sin created. In God, there are no gaps. God created both male and female in his image and likeness. God blessed both genders and gave them both equal dominion over everything on earth. He didn't tell Adam to work the field and Eve to gather the harvest and make dinner for him. It was sin—*sin!*—and the curse of sin that divided into two parts what God intended to be one whole and complete union.

When Christ was here on earth, he came to reveal the truth about the roles of women and men and redeem what sin had stolen in the garden. Through this brief encounter with Claudia, he reveals how godly relationships look. God takes those roles, those gaps, those consequences of sin and turns them into something for our good when we put him first like Claudia did. Because of this, we can't look at one gender and believe that it is a weaker vessel. We would, in fact, be saying to the triune God, some of your qualities are better than others, stronger than others, more holy than others, more revealing of your character than others, more beautiful than others, or more important than others. How could we ever say that to God?

But, Erin, isn't a woman supposed to be a *helper* to a man, to her husband? Ahhhh, so glad you asked.

God looked at Adam in the garden and said, "It is not good for man to be alone, I will make him a helper suitable" (Genesis 2:18, NIV).

The word "helper" in Genesis is used by God before he creates Eve. In Hebrew this word is *ezer*.[16] This same word, as it is used here, occurs twenty other times in the Old Testament. Once it's used when God makes Eve, and another time, when God raises up King David. Every other time this word is used, it refers to or about God, either as a plea for his help or in recognition of a time when he came to the psalmist's or Israelite's rescue.

For example, Psalm 70:5 states, "But as for me, I am poor and needy; please hurry to my aid, O God. You are my helper and my savior; O LORD, do not delay" (NIV).

In this passage, would you consider God's help weak?

In this verse and others like it, we see God bestowing help and coming to the rescue of those who are in need or those who are asking for aid. When they ask, God supernaturally comes, displaying his great love and mercy as he intervenes on their behalf. Doesn't this better explain the supernatural way he created Eve to help Adam?

He wasn't saying that Eve is a weaker vessel, created to help this great man. He also wasn't saying that Adam was weak and needed someone to help him get out of the messes he would inevitably make. *No!* They were still perfect in his sight and without sin or fault. Adam fully displayed God's glory. Eve fully displayed God's glory.

What I believe God was saying then and is still echoing to us today is that what he's imparted in the creation of each individual displays just one facet of his glory. I am one representation of his full glory. You are one representation of his full glory. Isn't it funny how it's always all about the Lord, and so often, we make it about ourselves?

The reason for our creation is to receive and reveal his glory. With the creation of man and woman in unity, our Creator was showing us that together, we more fully declare God's glory. Together.

We are to reflect the image and likeness of God for the benefit of each other. I better understand the nature of God when I look at my husband or at our children because the very nature of God is relational in union.

Didn't you know the Father more fully when you read about Jesus? Don't you understand the Word better when the Holy Spirit reveals it to you? Don't you believe more wholly in the power of the Holy Spirit when you understand the supremacy of Yahweh? They reflect and complete each other. You understand more of one because of the other. This greater understanding takes you from glory to glory to glory. (See 2 Corinthians 3:18.) We as men and women were designed to mirror this dynamic relationship.

When Pontius Pilate was weak, Claudia came in strong. She did try to help her husband with her revelation, wisdom and voice. Whether he heeded it or not, she revealed the glory of the Lord.

Within the walls of churches across this country and in countries around the world, we have turned gender issues into arguments when they are actually born of our own spiritual ignorance. Sweet Jesus, I believe this so much! If we would simply rise together, give one another space to be who God has called us to be, we would see marked, passionate change in the world for the gospel. Just please, don't take my word for it, *read your Bible.* It's right there! Jesus's heart and prayer on earth was to see unity come.

> I pray for them *all* to be joined together as one even as you and I, Father, are joined together as one. I pray for them to become one with us so that the world will recognize that you sent me. For the very glory you have given to me I have given them so that they will be joined together as one and experience the same unity we enjoy. You live fully in me and now I live fully in them so that they will experience perfect unity, and the world will be convinced that you have sent me, for they will see that you love each one of them with the same passionate love that you have for me (John 17:21–23, emphasis added).

What does this look like? It looks like what Jesus did with Mary Magdalene. She was likely a woman of high position and money. But her status here in this earthly kingdom was of little importance to Jesus. He saw the desolation in her spirit. Mary Magdalene had worked out her faith in the

Messiah after she was delivered of seven demons. As a result, she and a few other women followed Jesus and supported his ministry with their own means. Now those were some independent women!

Mary Magdalene was a devoted follower of Jesus. She was there on the day Jesus was crucified and buried. She was also there on the third day. She got up before the sun rose, put together spices and oil to anoint his body, and walked to the tomb where her Savior lay. Women cared for the bodies of their deceased as a common custom. Jesus used this cultural tradition to position her to bear witness to the greatest miracle of all times.

**She didn't let questions or fear disqualify her. She obeyed. Her obedience led her to an experience with Jesus unlike anyone else's.**

Mary was up early, working out her faith, wrestling with her unbelief, clinging to hope, striving, searching, and desiring Jesus. The men stayed back—distraught, fearful, and grieving, but she rose and went to serve Jesus, even in his death. Even when it seemed hopeless, even in her fear, even in her suffering. She. Went. She kept drawing near to him even when it didn't make sense.

When she arrived at the tomb, it was empty. (See John 20:1–8.) Jesus was risen, but she was confused. She ran to tell the others that Jesus's body was missing, to tell them that an angel appeared to her. They didn't believe her. They came to see for themselves, but their discovery only fueled more confusion. They left feeling even more hopeless, I bet. Mary, bewildered, cried at the tomb alone. That's when Jesus asked her why she was crying, not once but twice.

I love this. I must ask this question to at least one of my three girls daily. "Ella, Myla, Cecelia, why are you crying?" Though I'm sure I don't ask nearly as tenderly as Jesus asked Mary.

In the midst of our tears, we often don't know that the battle has been won. We don't realize Jesus is alive, near, and in love with us. He finally speaks her name, and when he does, she immediately recognizes his voice.

I can't wait to hear Jesus speak my name out loud. I hear it through the Holy Spirit, but to audibly hear it will just be explosive. I imagine that in this setting, it had the same effect when he spoke her name.

When she saw him, she bowed before him, worshipped him, and grabbed his feet. In return, Jesus gave her a purpose: a new job, a new order, and a new role. It came as she knelt, submitted, and listened *to Jesus*. He first said, "Don't be afraid." Next, he commanded her, "Go and tell my brothers— tell the men—that I'm alive, that you've seen me."

Mary did just that. She headed back to Galilee to tell the others what she had seen. She didn't let questions or fear disqualify her. She obeyed. Her obedience led her to an experience with Jesus unlike anyone else's. She was the first person to hear and see the resurrected King: not Peter (Jesus's closest friend), not John (the disciple Jesus loved), not his brothers, not the other Gospel writers, not Stephen who would be the first martyr, but Mary—an unwed, scandalous, forgiven, and freed woman.

Why? Because even in her grief, even though Jesus was dead, she kept drawing closer to him, she kept hoping, even when she didn't understand. Her purpose was to go, to tell what she had seen and heard. Then to tell others to find Jesus and experience him for themselves. That is your purpose, and that is my purpose, whether you are Mary or Peter or Moses or you with your list of disqualifications. Go and tell.

Your gender does not negate your purpose. It was specifically chosen to unleash it. Since this was the last place Jesus spoke to a woman and the last command he gave to one, why would we now think that Jesus would change his mind and want all women to be silent? Because his command is still the same today, no matter your gender. Go and tell.

Mary runs to tell them. She has walked with these men. She has experienced Jesus with them. She has seen his miracles, heard his messages, and seen him die, just like they have. And they have seen Jesus work miracles in her and seen her faithfulness in following him. I imagine she assumes this conversation should go well. She shares her experience, but in response, they call her crazy. Some call her words nonsense. Some just can't believe it. I imagine they rolled their eyes and disqualified her. But their disregard of her didn't change the truth; it didn't change the experience; it didn't change her purpose. We cannot let the response of others in the going and the telling change the truth of our message, our experience with Jesus, or our purpose in his kingdom. But so often we do.

So what does walking in unity together as brothers and sisters look like in practical terms? We see a great example in the book of Esther. King Xerxes reigns as a powerful ruler. At a party with his friends, he summoned his wife, Queen Vashti. She didn't want to come to him that night. Maybe she was too tired. Whatever the reason, she didn't go when the king called for her and committed a monumental offense, leading to a deadly fate. Xerxes now needed a new wife.

It turned out, a Jewish man named Mordecai could see something in his brave and beautiful cousin, Esther, she couldn't see in herself. He trained, encouraged, and championed her for this position as queen. Throughout the entire book of Esther, they relied on prayer and each other. Their unity served to stop an assassination attempt of the king, the total annihilation of the Jews, and the murder of Mordecai himself. They trusted each other through dire circumstances. And together, they focused on serving the king. When Esther doubted her position or her favor, Mordecai reminded her that she was born for such a time as this: to be strong and courageous.

(See Esther 4:14.)

This, friends, is how the relationship between men and women of God should look. Whether you are Esther or Mordecai, don't be flippant about the privileges you've been given in the kingdom. Mordecai used his influence to stand boldly on her behalf. What would the church look like if we did the same? How would God's glory be more evident?

One night, as my editor and I were feverishly running toward home plate to finish this book. In the midst of the madness, it was as if my sweet hubby had been reading these words. He knew full well the toll that birthing this book was taking on me. The life around me didn't stop just because my efforts were spent on something else. So he made dinner and ensured all the kids had baths and showers. He then cleaned the bathrooms while I read them books and tucked them into bed. He said, "I know this has been hard for you and how much messes stress you out. You're almost done. You can do it."

Hello, Mordecai. ☺

This is the simplest way we can help others live out the gospel. My husband could put a mop in my hand because he knows I like a tidy home. But he would be limiting my gifts. Instead he put a pen in it and encouraged me to use it. He knows the call on my life. He looks at me the way Jesus does.

Like Claudia, Mary Magdalene, Esther, and Mordecai, married or not, you have a position, relationships, and an influence that was provided by God. I pray you will take the risks in those places. Take risks whether your words fall on deaf ears or everyone is listening, whether they don't change the outcome or they change everything, whether they seem acceptable to everyone else or are deemed unacceptable, whether you're the only one speaking out or you're one voice in a unified front. Speak. He hears your voice and sees your choice. He is waiting for you, and *he* is listening.

## LET'S REFLECT:

If you knew your voice was valuable to Jesus, the church, and the advancing of God's kingdom, what would you say?

What are your beliefs about women in the church? Are there any exceptions to women holding leadership roles? Are there any ifs, ands, or buts?

How have you championed the voice of the oppressed? What are some ways you dream about doing that?

IT WON'T BE LONG UNTIL YOU
PART THE SKY

BUT TODAY YOU'RE CALLING SONS AND
DAUGHTERS TO ARISE

AND CARRY HOPE INTO THE
DARKEST NIGHT.

**"COME"**

**VALLEY'S END**

# ADVENTURE

**CHAPTER 13**

In the midst of ending one marriage and before embarking on another, I went to Maui. It was a freeing trip for me in many ways. The perfectionism of my life had unraveled. I had gone to Maui with Mickey against my parent's wishes and in the face of their disappointment, a decision for which I would later seek forgiveness.

One of the days we were there, we went to Ka'anapali Beach. Just off the shoreline is a three-mile lava formation known as Black Rock. Throughout the day, visitors can take in the beautiful scenery surrounding this heavenly place, and they can observe the most breathtaking sight: cliff divers.

I watched these courageous souls for several hours—jumping, diving, some with arms and legs flailing as they fell—and decided that I could do it too. What was the worst thing that could happen? I could seriously injure myself or someone else. I could be maimed for life. I could die. All possible. But I had watched forty or fifty people go already, and no one had come close to meeting any of those fates. What made them different from me?

They looked ordinary enough. So I said goodbye to Mickey, who looked at me as if I had lost my mind. He had no desire to go. I swam over to the infamous Black Rock.

I watched several individuals go ahead of me. They were moving with the rhythm of the sea. When the wave came in, the water carried them far enough above the stepping stone to land on top of it, a place you couldn't get to without the help of the water. I didn't realize this until I scratched my knee on the lava rock while attempting to climb it in my own strength. Waiting for the water to rise was essential. Once atop this rock, the climb to the pinnacle of the jumping-off point was less rigorous but much more terrifying. Falling during this climb would certainly cause injury or death. I kept my eyes on the people ahead of me and the path before me. I couldn't turn back now. I was locked in. There was no way out but to jump. I was at the top, watching the waves, counting the rhythm in order to jump when the water was at the optimum level. I waved at Mickey, who was readying a plan for recovering my body. I threw up a superficial prayer. "Lord, let me hit water only." And I jumped thirty feet into the crisp Pacific water, screaming the whole way down.

**Tear out every page where he's not the God who does impossible things. Set that page on fire and start asking him to do things we could never do without him.**

Unbelievable freedom came when I plunged into the water and popped up. It was crazy invigorating and unearthed courage I didn't know I had. The endeavor and the leap released a contagious joy. So contagious that Mickey decided if I could do it, he could too. He was joyful in the midst of the unknown because of what he saw me do.

Even in the middle of my sin, even when I hadn't sought forgiveness,

God used my abandon for my good. He was already writing this story. Taking back these memories and inscribing them into his story for me. When I remember this moment, my memory is surrounded with joy. Just like that jump, the joy comes from knowing that the journey we are embarking on from our perspective seems impossible. It is so reckless and unbelievable that we have to surrender our lives to the adventure. It's in the surrender, the yes, the agreement with God, that the joy is released, because truly, that's the first leap we take.

Impossible is God's favorite place to work. In fact, he's always inviting us to pursue the impossible with him. He's inviting us to tear out the page of our own agenda. Tear out the page where our thoughts are not his thoughts. The page where he is small and all that we're asking for is safety. Tear out every page where he's not the God who does impossible things. Set that page on fire and start asking him to do things we could never do without him.

Oswald Chambers describes the unearthing I've experienced in this impossible adventure with him:

> Again, I want to emphasize the fact that the teaching of Jesus Christ does not appear as first to be what it truly is. At first it appears to be beautiful and pious and lukewarm—but before long it becomes a ripping and tearing torpedo that splits to atoms every preconceived notion a person ever had.[17]

I could've stayed on the shore of Maui's Ka'anapali Beach on that perfect September day. The view was beautiful from the shoreline too. I could've explained all the ways one could jump off Black Rock and assume I understood how it felt to dive from that spot. I could've even guessed that it was easy, because, from my vantage point, it sure looked easy. But I believed that jumping from that rock was as much an invitation to me as it was to anyone else who jumped. Receiving the invitation in my soul, I said yes. As you've already read, it was soon after that, I would say yes to God's invitation to come home to him. Since then, the Bible continues to rip and tear apart every preconceived notion I ever had about God before actually getting to know him.

Now that I know him, I long to do what he did. I want to take him at his word. So many of his words sound like opportunities for new adventures. When I hear Jesus saying, "Go," all these times in the Gospels, I become so excited to follow him. It feels as if we're about to take a trip. Perfect! I love to travel. I love exploring new cultures, experiencing new landscapes, and braving new foods.

My first-ever plane ride was by myself in the seventh grade. I had an invitation from my aunt to visit her and my cousin in the mountains of New Mexico. My parents walked me to the gate at the airport. They calmed my fears by explaining, "Honey, that whole plane is safe because you're on it." They taught me how to find my connecting flight in Dallas, just in case an airline representative forgot me and sent me off. That was the first of many firsts I would experience as a traveler.

As the third-born in a family of independent children, it was hard to find something that I could do before anyone else had already been there and done that. But traveling was my escape from all my other easily observable traits. This was a love in my heart, a joy knit into me, that you would only learn about once you got to know me.

This love of travel served me well when I was in high school as I took my first mission trip to Guatemala. This trip connected my love for other cultures with a deep desire to share the love of Jesus. Two years later, a trip to Juarez, Mexico, sealed a desire within me to be a missionary in any domestic and/or foreign fields the Lord provided.

Before I came back from my first mission trip, my parents sat everyone down and explained, "Okay, your sister is going to come back and tell us she wants to be a missionary. I'm sure she'll explain that she had a life-changing trip. Just let her talk. Don't ask her too many questions about how or when. Most teenagers say stuff like that after a trip like this."

I never did get over it. My husband and I are now leaders of the Missions and Outreach ministry at our church. I don't quite know how this happened except that a trip to Haiti came up, and we raised our hands high! Our eagerness seemed to answer the prayers of our beloved missions' pastor who, unbeknownst to us, was preparing to retire. Six months later, during that trip, in a dark, concrete classroom, our missions' pastor offered to pass the torch to us. "Do you feel the Lord calling you?" he asked. We nodded yes with tears streaming down our faces.

Before my first trip to Haiti, a dear friend said, "I know you're going to have the best time. It's like it's woven into the very fiber of who you are to go." She was right. Adventure with Jesus is what I'm about, messy and beautiful adventure. It's wild and wonderful and feels like home and heaven.

In the following passage, Jesus's parting words to us were an invitation. More than that, they were a declaration of adventure over us. This commissioning qualifies us to join him in bringing heaven to earth. How cool is that?

"I will give you the keys of heaven's kingdom realm to forbid on earth that which is forbidden in heaven, and to release on earth that which is released in heaven" (Matthew 16:19 TPT).

"Then Jesus came close to them and said, 'All the authority of the universe has been given to me. Now go *in my authority* and make disciples of all nations, baptizing them in the name of the Father, the Son, and the Holy Spirit. And teach them to faithfully follow all that I have commanded you. And never forget that I am with you every day, even to the completion of this age" (Matthew 28:18–20).

Before I could operate in this authority—making disciples and baptizing and teaching and adventuring that's bestowed to us—I had to stop and surrender all the ways I had misunderstood these verses. *All* authority in heaven and on earth has been given to *me?* And with all the authority that has been given to me, *this* is what he asks me to do? I wanted to understand what all this meant.

Jesus was serious in what he was commissioning us to do. Just because he's serious doesn't mean there's not joy in it. In fact, joy is supposed to be our motivation for whatever we do for the kingdom. It's not *for* him. It's because of him and with him.

Remember my friend, Faye from Haiti, with the knotted jump rope? A second part of that story bears telling.

See, after I untangled the rope and handed it back to a beaming Faye, I began to bend down to gather up my things, thinking she would run off and play. Instead, she held the plastic end up to my face and in her beautiful, accented English, said, "You play?"

I couldn't hide the tears any longer; they were fogging up my sunglasses and streaming down my neck, mixing with all the sweat that Haiti brings. She didn't just want me for the moment that was outside her control. She wanted me to play. Her love for me was real. Her trust in me was true. I wasn't just a tool she could use to help unknot her problems; she knew I would delight in her joy. We had played this game together before. She was inviting me to swing the rope, count the jumps, sing a rhyming song to her, and ensure that she didn't get pushed around by other kids who wanted to play too.

Many of us miss adventure and fun in our relationship with the Lord. But truly, it's the abundant life he's offered to us. What good is freedom if we still act like slaves, if we find no joy in the freedom we have found? If we wear suffering like a burden?

My Lord and Savior untangled all the knots I'd worked into my life in the midnight hours, in my driveway, in the early morning, while I was playing with my kids, while I was cooking, or writing over the course of many years. I knew I could trust him. All he ever wanted for me was freedom. All he wants for me now is freedom. I've arrived at this place, yet I'm still arriving. Understanding this, I knew if I carried that rope without him, I would surely lose it or tangle it up again. It would get stolen, and/or it just wouldn't be as fun playing by myself. So I put it back in his hands and asked if he wanted to play with me. What every kid is always asking is, "Can we play?"

In God's kingdom, he is always adventuring, always down for fun, always inventing new games, always dancing, always experiencing joy in his work, always releasing some mind-blowing miracle. Whenever my kids see me having fun, they ask to play with me. The Lord was showing me, through sweet, doe-eyed Faye, that the most fun I've ever had and will ever have comes from asking Jesus to play. My life is best in his hands with him holding the rope and keeping the rhythm. All I have to do is jump for joy. And when I do, just as happened with Faye and me that day, others see us playing and ask to join in too.

As Mickey and I have been adventuring with the Lord, it's as if each time we take our time to just delight in him, he hands us another treasure map that leads to his promises, like an Indiana Jones adventure. My favorite. The treasure map he has given us is the Bible just like Indiana Jones followed a guide map given to him by his father. And off screen, though unseen by Indy, his father is whispering the answers to encourage faith and reveal hidden truths.

In the scene after the penitent, kneeling man, Indiana Jones is standing before a great chasm known as *The Path of God*. It is so wide and deep that he could not leap across it. Viewed only with his earthly eyes, Indy is filled with doubt, afraid to move ahead. "This is impossible," he surmises.

"Nobody could jump across this."

But in the background, his father encourages him toward faith. "Just believe, my son."

Indy reads his father's book again. He is assured that this is the only escape from impending doom. His mind fights to agree with the faith that is compelling his heart. Finally his father's words settle into him, and he understands that this is a leap of faith. The chasm is so wide that faith must drive his next steps lest he and his family both suffer the same fate.

**My friend, we are now the Bible people. Step out in faith. Throw the sand. It's the most fun!**

He puts down the book, surveys what he cannot see before him, closes his eyes, and grabs his chest, mustering up courage to believe in what his father has written. He's hoping he interpreted it correctly. With his eyes closed, he puts out his foot to step into the unknown. Down he plummets until the nothingness materializes underneath his feet, creating a bridge to the Cup of Promise. Joy and relief fill him. Purpose and resolve determine his steps as he begins to trust his father's book. Hope propelled what faith revealed.

And then my favorite part occurs: As he moves into the cave on the other side of the bridge, he turns, takes some of the dirt from under his feet, and throws it over the invisible bridge. He doesn't want to forget about the bridge. He doesn't want to learn the same lesson twice. He wants to be able to quickly return to offer the cup of healing to others.

Goodness, I love that imagery! The Bible is made up of people just like us who threw sand over the invisible God to make what is unseen, seen.

My friend, we are now the Bible people. Step out in faith. Throw the sand. It's the most fun!

In 2010, my dear friend, Mariangel, was going through an identity crisis similar in feeling, not circumstance, to what I had just gone through. She knew who Jesus was but didn't have any kind of relationship with him. She had known me pre-divorce and now, newly married, with two little babies. Newly single and living nearby, she would come over often and ask me questions or tell me stories about her life. Our friendship was growing, I just loved spending time with her.

In church one Sunday, while I was praising Jesus in my seat, she was heavy on my heart. I closed my eyes to pray for her. I knew I needed to sing the lyrics over her. As soon as I closed my eyes, I had a vision of her standing in complete darkness. Her eyes were looking straight ahead, almost dead, somehow tormented. The terrible darkness on one side of her was warring for her, pulling her toward it. On the other side was light: full, beautiful, and powerful light, fighting the darkness, protecting her against any further gains. I was overwhelmed, shaking, and crying. I had never seen anything like it. I knew the stakes for her life were steep. I knew the next time I saw her, I had to share Jesus with her as afraid as I was of offending her and of costing me our friendship. (Disclaimer: You do not need to have this kind of vision to introduce people to hope.)

Just a few days later, she came over to my house for dinner with my crazy little crew. She seemed more desperate than usual. She was pacing, uncertain, and insecure. She looked the least like herself that I had ever seen. We talked around and about many different subjects. I just wanted to disregard the disturbing vision I had seen because I felt ill-equipped to share the gospel with her. I felt ordinary. My thoughts were wreaking havoc on my own beliefs in the power of grace and salvation. The time was flying by, and she headed for the door, thanking me for dinner. Finally I blurted out, "You don't seem like you have any peace"—she turned, and

183

I knew I had her attention—"well, peace can only be found through Jesus." I cringed, leaving one eye half-open, waiting for her response.

To my utter disbelief and surprise, she replied, "I don't know what that looks like." Hmmm, wonder why? I painted the perfect picture, didn't I? Ha!

I put down the dishes. We moved toward the couch, and I explained, "I'd be happy to tell you."

That night, just a few hours later, she accepted Jesus Christ as her Lord and Savior while my kids and husband were asleep upstairs. In my eagerness, I woke up everyone with my joy. I called my parents, my brother, and my sister at, like, midnight.

My mom reminded me, "Now the discipleship begins."

Wait, what?

I freaked. I lay in my bed, wondering what this meant for my well-structured life, my tightly planned schedule, my bursting agenda, my packed nights and weekends, *my* precious time. How much would this cost me? I felt totally inept. These thoughts stole joy right out from under me during one of the most amazing experiences of my life! I looked at this process as a must-do instead of a made-to.

Through recognizing that I am a daughter of a King, I've learned that I've been uniquely designed. I've been given authority and a voice to proclaim the gospel of Jesus, because of this my comfort takes a backseat. A true heir understands more than the power they wield; they consider the responsibility they've been given. The problem is that in Christian circles, we take this authority for granted and hope instead for our ticket out of here soon. We neglect this world and the people in it in every way imaginable.

We are seeking a rapture from the responsibility we've been given to tend the garden God has entrusted us with on this earth, both the literal soil of the ground we stand on and the metaphorical soil of human hearts because we know farming is hard work.

Currently, the hubs and I are engaged in an eighty-day workout program. Every day, I think, *How terrible and awful this is.* And because I'm constantly sore, this is the cry of my heart nearly every time I stand, sit, go to the bathroom, or move one muscle even an inch. When I move, it hurts. This is some kind of demented system of justice over my body. Things need to face resistance before they grow. It doesn't make logical sense, but it's true. Everything develops under resistance through perseverance. The light resisted the darkness when God spoke the words on the first day of creation. Both righteousness and unrighteousness fall under this law of sowing and reaping. It's not just fruits, grains, and veggies. Gracious God, I could never be a farmer. We have had gardens before, and I still cannot understand this patient, beautiful work. Oh, the uncomfortable life of a farmer.

**I lay in my bed, wondering what this meant for my well-structured life, my tightly planned schedule, my bursting agenda, my packed nights and weekends, my precious time.**

What are they made of? How can they stand this? How do they not become weary when they've gone through seasons of famine, disease, bureaucracy, scarcity, and drought? So I asked God, "Is it just in their DNA to persevere with joy and endure with patience?" Yes. And it's in yours too. Made in the image of God, we have been given patience; we can develop endurance; we can persevere with joy! These qualities are spiritually gifted to us as they are practiced, walked out, and tested with faith.

"But that's not all! Even in times of trouble we have a joyful confidence, knowing that our pressures will develop in us patient endurance" (Romans 5:3).

But something comes to steal our joyful confidence, doesn't it? It's the enemy. He wants to rip what we've planted out of the ground. He longs to sow seeds of doubt, unbelief, immorality, selfishness, and every other form of evil. And I think it's because we forget who he really is that we give him so much attention. Because if we really understood that our God is faithful, diligent, and patient, oh, how it would change our perspective with our gardens with every season of advancing the kingdom as the Body of Christ. See, God is in it for the long game. But this enemy that we give so much credit to is not in it for the long game. He is a short-term resident here. So he's not built for patience like we are. He gives up. He is not faithful. His work doesn't endure. It falls away. We will outpace him in patience, in faithfulness, and endurance Every. Single. Time. If we just don't give up.

C.S. Lewis eloquently explains our difficulty with endurance to Mr. Wormwood in *The Screwtape Letters*:

> As spirits they belong to the eternal world, but as animals they inhabit time. This means that while their spirit can be directed to an eternal object, their bodies, passions and imaginations are in continual change, for to be in time means to change. Their nearest approach to constancy, therefore, is undulation—the repeated return to a level from which they repeatedly fall back, a series of troughs and peaks...As long as he lives on earth periods of emotional and bodily richness and liveliness will alternate with periods of numbness and poverty.[18]

We undulate and waver through our commitment to the church. Our ministry obstructs our faith; at times, our singularity with God obstructs our work to actually live out our faith. We obsess over the feeling we first had with him at a conference or in a special moment, and we believe we are in a period of dryness. We believe he has left us, and we forget, as we do, that we are not meant to live as feeling vessels first. We are not meant to put faith in our feelings or in our intellect. We measure them according to the truth of our salvation through Jesus Christ, who felt every physical and emotional pain and still called out for our forgiveness.

He didn't allow the back and forth of the mind, will, and emotions (the soul) dictate his response to endure. He pleaded and prayed with cries and tears to the one who could rescue him from death for endurance on the cross and "learned obedience from the things he suffered." (See Hebrews 5:7–8.) He suffered and endured for our sakes. He could've revolted. He could've called down the heavenly hosts. He could've condemned us all. But he didn't. He let love endure and bring healing.

Oh, friends, hear me. We have robbed people of seeing the marvel, wonder, and innocence of faith because we haven't cared enough to foster it in our own lives. They need to know that we have tasted and seen that the Lord is good—not a fading good, either. He's an all-the-time-and-forever-more good. We have to let them see that we are so passionate about freedom, that we're not afraid to talk about what kept us in bondage, whether it was perfectionism, vice, or both. Only free people can speak so openly and directly. You don't have to do that because you experienced captivity and are now free; you can do it just by understanding that imperfect people are imprisoned in a jail cell, repaying debts that were already pardoned. Go tell them they don't have to live there anymore. And when you do, the generations before and after you will be inspired to do the same.

Jesus told us to be ready. He taught us to pray, "Set us free from evil," so that temptation wouldn't have a grip on our lives. We have to be discipled in these truths by the Word of God through the Holy Spirit and by mentors who are rooted in faith and grace who long to see the generation before them go further in the kingdom of God than they did. We can't create a place for the enemy to lie to us about our worth, to let us compare. Put your big kid pants on and kick that liar out! It's costing us a unified and passionate church.

We have to stop letting our fears, our doubts, our comfort, and our laziness keep our love from acting as just a theological concept of our faith. We have to become uncomfortable. We have to. We're not meant to do it all right; we're just meant to do it. His love pours into you so that you will pour it out. You were made to love, which means that it will get messy and might even hurt. And that's why we don't want to do it. Loving like Jesus is unpredictable and muddled and selfless and uncomfortable. Loving like that takes courage and strength that we don't have within ourselves.

If you're a middle-class American like me, you might cringe at some of these words. We've gotten too good at being in control, at keeping the mess at bay, at turning the channel, at sleeping through the fire, at tunnel vision. What a privilege that is, and that privilege has caused us to become the land of the free and the home of the comfortable. Friends, I've got news for ya. We were called to get uncomfortable.

In the Garden of Gethsemane, just before Jesus was betrayed and arrested, he brought three of the disciples over to pray for him. When he walked away, they laid down and got comfortable, eventually falling asleep. Jesus came over to wake them, asking:

"Do you lack the strength to stay awake with me for even just an hour? Keep alert and pray that you'll be spared from this time of testing. You should have learned by now that your spirit is eager enough, but your humanity is weak" (Matthew 26:40b–41).

This should've caused them to rise and begin to pray, but Jesus caught them sleeping *again*. I know we are comfortable because that is our humanity, our flesh, our nature. We want to find the path of least resistance and enjoy it.

Jesus is waking us up. He's saying, "Don't you know by now that you can't trust your humanity? Your spirit knows the truth and is eager to obey, so ask the Holy Spirit to come and strengthen your flesh to keep alert so that you can continue the good work of love I've called you to." Jesus asks the Father to do exactly this for him. And in that moment, when he asked for the Father's help, the Bible says angels came to strengthen him.

He's given us the key and the way to stay woke in every sense of the word: through prayer and the power of the Holy Spirit.

I had woken up my mom with my middle-of-the-night phone call. But who was really waking who up? When my mom jolted me awake with the truth about discipleship, I

**We've gotten too good at being in control, at keeping the mess at bay, at turning the channel, at sleeping through the fire, at tunnel vision. What a privilege that is, and that privilege has caused us to become the land of the free and the home of the comfortable.**

had to count the cost. (See Luke 14:28.) Jesus says that's a wise thing to do because you don't know everything it will involve. But you can't separate the cost from the fruit, the reward, the joy. I couldn't know then that I would be the one to baptize her in my pool, drive her up to Washington, D.C., move her there when she accepted a new job, answer the phone when she called in the middle of the night, and cling to my Bible and the wisdom of the Holy Spirit through her thousands of questions over the years. Even if I had known all that, I certainly couldn't have fathomed that this would be one of the most rewarding relationships of my life.

In Matthew 28, Jesus told us to make disciples twice. First, bring them into the kingdom, then teach them about the kingdom. (See vs. 19–20.) He knew this would take an earthly lifetime. What's the reward for this? I have gained an eternal friend. She is one of my dearest friends, one who I can call now when I need prayer. One who has prayed for me through every chapter of this book. I hope Jesus puts our houses on the same street in heaven.

Ya know what? I wish I could tell you that "going with Jesus" always ends like this. It doesn't. Sometimes people look at me weird. There are friends I've lost in the process. I've cried more tears for my friends and family, for orphans, the poor, the least, the lost, the broken, than I could ever count. But heaven knows. Heaven cries those tears too. Heaven keeps every tear like it's a valuable prayer. No matter the tears, my hope is still in Jesus. Hope is what we cling to when we're tired of these pilgrim days.

In 2017, Mickey and I went on our first trip to Haiti, a country we had no idea we would love so much. We toured the city with Daniel, a friend to our team and a local minister there. As we drove in a paddy wagon, a box truck with a caged back door, through the slums in the city of Soleil and the forgotten earthquake rubble of Port au Prince, I asked him, "What do you feel when you see the country you love in a state like this?"

"Hopeful," he said, "because of Jesus." And suddenly, so did I. I felt renewed hope for both our countries, in fact. Because we suffer the same without it. But it wasn't just the country I felt hope for. It was my friend and others like him.

On that first trip, we brought gifts and love to the children as we slept in the missionary quarters on the floor just above their bunks. We went to the local school where the children were educated each day; we opened the doors and invited the community to hear the gospel through VBS. I was so honored to have an opportunity to speak to the local church on Sunday. As I went to sleep the night before, the palm trees were blowing in the wind outside the porthole window of our room. We regularly see the same image—palm trees blowing in the breeze—in our neck of the woods in Florida. As I stared, I remembered how Jerusalem ushered in Jesus on Palm Sunday. They were waving their palm branches, singing:

"Hosanna in the Highest! Blessed is he who comes in the name of the Lord." (See John 12:12–13.)

It was a symbol, an image that I could cling to, a reminder that we had everything in common because the hope we have for both our nations propels us to continue the work we are doing, proclaiming the coming of the Lord. We both needed reminding because it's uncomfortable, diligent work. The Western world could easily borrow the hope they are clinging to because our souls lean toward resting in our own accomplishments. The Haitians could just as easily welcome the Western world into their modest, desperate places and borrow the resources we have in vast quantities. This would be the most simple and obvious exchange. But I knew that we were there for more. So the Lord showed me this:

*We are family. More connects us than separates us. Let's be honest about the hope we've put in each other instead of in Yahweh. Let's be honest about what we're after. And then, remember we are united in Christ. We are both, in different ways, living in a dry and weary land. Though we are living in a desolate place, we have not been deserted. We are both seen by our Father.*

Even this year, as we worked to build broken-down bunkbeds for the orphans, we did it alongside our Haitian brothers and sisters. As we stay connected from home, we know their struggles don't end after we leave. We're not going to look away. We're going to stay linked, arm in arm, because being with them honors them, shows them respect, tempers my need to fix things, and allows me to be present in their poverty and in my abundance. That's a tough place to stay; guilt knocks regularly on that door. But my rich, white guilt doesn't benefit anyone either.

When escape from this tension tempts me, I am reminded of a song that I heard there that still lingers in my ears. This song rang so clearly in my soul that I thought it had certainly been written just for my ears, just for this summer night in a concrete church with no doors and no evidence of the kinds of walls I know how to build. It was a simple lyric, a simple message of hope, with a depth that continues to soothe and comfort the ache in my heart. This song brought the teeter of hope I needed with this word:

*N'ap Avanse* (Nah-paw-vawn-say). It means: We advance.

See, whether with two or twelve or a hundred or five thousand, whether the progress is evident or hidden, in our faithfulness, N'ap Avanse.

When honesty about our differences leads to repentance and embrace. When we know what we do and when we don't know what we do, in our confession, N'ap Avanse.

When we realize that we are the same. Our desires for our children, our love for our families, our joy in song, and our frustration in human weakness is not isolated to our own nation or people. But we are of the same Spirit, clinging to the same truth, pouring out the same love, living in the same hope, in our unity, N'ap Avanse.

When both our lands seem desperate and dry, and our hearts are broken beyond words. When the need is great, in our prayers for both Americans and for Haitians, in the name of Jesus, N'ap Avanse.

In these pilgrim days, N'ap Avanse.

My friends, because we've partnered with the Almighty God in this daring adventure, we advance.

## LET'S REFLECT:

Think of a person in your life who is strong in faith but humble enough to admit the areas where they struggle. Consider reaching out to begin a mentoring or accountability relationship.

In what ways do you fear deep relationships and the time and investment they might take?

Have you ever considered life with Jesus to be an adventure? Why or why not?

How would your adventure with Jesus look different from mine?

FOR YOUR DANCING PARTNER YOU
HAVE CHOSEN ME

SUDDENLY MY SPIRIT IS AWAKENING

IT'S TOO LATE TO CONCENTRATE
SO I'LL JUST BE.

**"DANCING WITH MY KING"**

**VALLEY'S END**

# YOU'RE INVITED

**CHAPTER 14**

From the time I was little until now, whenever I accomplished something above and beyond what my mom had accomplished, she lovingly reminded me in her soothing and admiring prayer voice, "Honey, where I walked, may you run." Isn't that just like a loving parent? They feel no regret or jealousy in their hearts for their children's accomplishments. They always want you to go further and faster than they did.

It is a joy for me to watch my oldest write story after story. I don't admonish or stifle her gifts when she misspells a word or doesn't use any punctuation. I know she'll learn all that. And when she does, she'll love to write all the more because her thoughts will be clear, focused, and understood. I don't want her to shrink back from using her gifts, and it is my joy as a mom to invite and encourage her to use them even when unpolished.

Guess who parents us that way?

Yep, our heavenly Father.

I don't understand why I—we—struggle to believe that God's plans for us are so much greater than what we could accomplish on our own.

In John 14:12–13, Jesus tells the disciples, "I tell you the truth, anyone who believes in me will do the same works I have done, and even greater works, because I am going to be with the Father. 13 You can ask for anything in my name, and I will do it, so that the Son can bring glory to the Father" (NLT).

Now this seems like crazy talk. But I have learned that crazy, humble, love kind of talk is Jesus talk. It raises so many questions in our minds, doesn't it? Um, Jesus? Are you sure about this because, well, you're *Jesus*! You are God with us! How can we do greater things than you did?

And please notice that this does not say we *are* greater than Jesus. No servant is above his master. He says you "will *do* even greater things than [he has] done."

That's because Jesus is always kingdom-focused through and through. He is modeling this in both speech and action. Jesus is teaching us, if it's a win for the kingdom, then it's a win for his name. When or if we are only looking to proclaim the freedom and love of Jesus, then whatever fame is received or adventure comes out of it is a direct result of fulfilling our purpose. It's a result of walking out of this kind of humility and surrender with him.

And the thing I love about this passage of Scripture is that if Jesus didn't say this to us, then he wouldn't be love in the flesh! He wouldn't be who he is! He has no pride, arrogance, or insecurity; otherwise he couldn't tell us this. But because he takes pride in us, his children, he invites us to do even greater things than he did. He gives these words to us, his disciples, so we wouldn't limit our faith in him.

Just like in the garden before he faced the cross, he's saying, "Keep alert and in prayer so that you'll be ready when your faith is tested, when people betray you, harm you, and hate you." We shouldn't think that we're only supposed to do what Jesus did. He wants us to think beyond what he did. He wants our faith in him to be ever-increasing. He doesn't want us to limit the reach of his hand.

In all this, he was preparing us, his disciples, to receive the Holy Spirit. "But very truly I tell you, it is for your good that I am going away. Unless I go away, the Advocate will not come to you; but if I go, I will send him to you" (John 16:7, NIV).

I bet they were really uncomfortable with this statement. I'm sure they thought, "How could it be better for you to go away and send us an Advocate?"

Because with the Advocate, we operate with the Spirit of God *in* us! Individually and collectively, we become the Body of Christ. We are unified in spirit and in truth. We can be set free and set other captives free. And if you can believe it, throughout eternity, this brief time on earth is the *only* place we'll be able to do that! Doesn't that invigorate you? Oh, man! It makes me so excited! Starting now and for eternity, I will be reveling in all the love, joy, and peace of Jesus. I will be joining all the believers in a unified and epic celebration of our King. That's forever my inheritance and yours as a believer.

Here on earth, we have this transitory opportunity to spread the good news! What are we so afraid of? This is all fleeting! Why are we so anxious to be raptured from responsibility, given that this is the only place where we will have the ability to challenge the invading darkness? I echo the sentiment of King David: What can mere mortals do to me? (See Psalm 118:6.)

The early church got this. The disciples would understand these powerful statements from Jesus because they would, in fact, do greater things than Jesus did during his ministry. Through the power of the Holy Spirit, they ministered to government leaders and kings. They were released from prison. They received revelation and wrote down the words of Jesus himself. They went into many nations. They spoke many languages. They performed miracles and saw many lives saved. These things needed to be done for the growth of the kingdom. He knows this, so he places desires in our hearts so that his will can be accomplished through us.

**I know this to be true of Jesus. I've experienced it. He's given me back me.**

Jesus has invited me on a lot of adventures. He's asked me over and over to go with him. To some, I've given a quick yes. To some, I've given a hard no. Most often, I'm afraid to admit, I agree reluctantly. It took me the longest to embark on the journey to write this book. But I'm certain, just like Solomon.

"I've made up my mind. Until the darkness disappears and the dawn has fully come, in spite of shadows and fears, I will go to the mountaintop with you—the mountain of suffering love and the hill of burning incense. Yes, I will be your bride" (Song of Songs 4:6).

Suffering love is not in vain. It's salvation's love. It's the love Jesus freely gives to us. When we respond to his love unto salvation with him, we're saying, "I'll go to the hill of Calvary with you, Lord. I will die to my own desires. I'll go willingly, no matter the difficulty. I'll climb the mountain with you."

When we read those statements and see death, difficulty, die, hill, go, and obedience, we become tired before we even begin. It's not that those statements aren't true; we just haven't experienced enough of Jesus to know that he is a fun adventurer, worth the risk.

Mary Poppins didn't invent the idea of enjoying your work, neither did the seven dwarves or Cinderella. This is a godly principle and inheritance. He gives us friendships and mentors to support and encourage us along the way. He gives us exciting and unique challenges that expand the framework of our own gifts, talents, and personality.

How do I know he'll do this? Because what does every loving parent say after a child asks them to play? The parent asks them, "What do *you* want to play?" When we invite Jesus into our lives, his response is to ask us about our dreams, passions, and talents. Why? Because he put them there.

∽ ♡ ∽

"Delight yourself also in the Lord, and He shall give you the desires of your heart. Commit your way to the Lord, trust also in Him, and He shall bring it to pass" (Psalm 37:4–5, NKJV).

C.S. Lewis reiterates it as follows in *The Screwtape Letters*:

Remember always, that He really likes the little vermin, and sets an absurd value on the distinctness of every one of them. When He talks of their losing their selves, He only means abandoning the clamour of self-will; once they have done that, He really gives them back all their personality, and boasts (I am afraid, sincerely) that when they are wholly His they will be more themselves than ever.[19]

I know this to be true of Jesus. I've experienced it. He's given me back me. So when he asked, "What do you want to play, Erin?" I was reminded of how much I have always loved to write. I was an English major in college and always knew that I wanted to write. I just wasn't sure how that would pan out. As the Lord began to talk to me about writing out this story in book form, I knew I didn't want to write a book that I could write. I wanted to write a book that only we could write together. Let's play, Jesus.

From my experience, this adventure has been so fun (sigh) until I become selfish and fearful. If I would just submit my questions, all the revelation would come for this adventure. But often, we're too afraid to ask questions. Or we've incorrectly believed God is angry at us for our humanness, our need for clarity, or reminding. Our problem is unbelief. I hold back; I don't yield or surrender what I hold so sacred. I don't offer it up even though he's invited me into the most sacred places. He's not kept anything from me. Why would I hold tightly to anything, even my unbelief, especially because the very nature of God ensures that he will care for it better than I will. Two reasons: I forget, and I can't fathom. Let's talk about them.

> At your worst, at your best, he loves you the same. We can't fathom this because we know ourselves better than we know him.

First, our forgetfulness must be the worst of all our faults. Jesus knew that we had this tendency, so he gave us the Bible, each other, and the Holy Spirit to remind us. Our ability to forget his Word, his way, his mercy, and his love for us created a need for him to be with us all the time. The Holy Spirit gives us a glimpse of what will someday be available to us forever, void of the humanness of ourselves, of all the ways we forget the goodness of our Savior. His constant presence with us can be uncomfortable.

Which leads me to our next point. We can't fathom that he would be kind even in our most stubborn places. It's the most confounding thing to believe that he could love me just as much now, surrendered and living for him, as he did when I was far away from him. How is that possible? But it's true. At your worst, at your best, he loves you the same. We can't fathom this because we know ourselves better than we know him.

At times, I have so doggedly barked at my children for a day or two over everything that they are sometimes afraid to ask me—their mom!—a question. One of my children doesn't scare as easily. She has spunk and isn't quick to back down. When I'm beyond frustrated at whatever mess we've gotten ourselves into that day, she will not relent in her pursuit for a reward she believes she's due. She believes these are separate issues.

She might say something like this. "You're mad at something. I can see that. I still ate all my vegetables. I cleared my plate and had mostly good manners. I am entitled to ice cream. Asking you for something I feel entitled to shouldn't make you so mad."

This beautiful girl of mine often surmises incorrectly. It does send me reeling even if it shouldn't. I'm human, and my love is conditional. Because this is a correct view of my humanness, I sometimes exchange this view of love for God's perfect, unconditional love. I become scared to approach him with doubts, scared away by my own unbelief. Why don't we believe that he finds our unbelief sacred? He shines his glory into this space, the intimate place where he renews our minds with his inconceivable love. We think he's saying, "Why do you forget, and why don't you understand?" But he's actually saying, "Come with me. I'll remind you of my love if you forget along the way. I'll explain the depths of my love whenever you don't understand." This is the adventure to which he invites us. Can I tell you the truth about something? We only have two answers. Yes or no. We either go with the Lord because we believe, or we don't go because we don't believe. When we refuse to go, we carelessly toss out his book of promises in our unbelief and disobedience.

Revivalist Leonard Ravenhill put it this way:

> One of these days some simple soul will pick up the Book of God,

read it, and believe it. Then the rest of us will be embarrassed. We have adopted the convenient theory that the Bible is a Book to be explained, whereas first and foremost it is a Book to be believed (and after that to be obeyed).[20]

Walking with Jesus works in the exact same way. The invitation is extended. It's the same for me as it is for you. If I believe it, if I believe in the God who wrote it, the Jesus who completed it, the Holy Spirit who reveals it, then I have to obey it. Not because of duty or a desire to be good, but because I so desperately want it to be proven true.

As seniors in high school, five of us had the same sociology teacher who worked as a forest ranger in Yellowstone National Park every summer. He would go early to clear hiking trails and ready the park for its busiest time of year. His family followed him up later in June, which made space in his cabin for us to join him to clear trails and learn the ways of being a park ranger. Does this seem like the beginning of a horror story? Every time I tell this tale, people look at me or my parents in terror.

I can assure you, it was as innocent as I describe. He sat with our parents and personally assured them of our safety. He truly loved his students and loved the great outdoors. He also loved McDonald's. I had him for first period my senior year, and his agreement with several students was that he would not count tardies against us if we brought him an Egg McMuffin. According to my calculations, this cost me about $200.00 as I was late several times per week.

A few days after my high school graduation the last week in May, we flew to Salt Lake City, drove up to the west entrance of Yellowstone, and stayed for ten days. During that time, we explored the waters, trails, and wonder of one of the most beautiful places on earth.

Mid-week we embarked on a journey north to the entrance at Fawn Pass. It was an eighteen-mile roundtrip hike that climbed two thousand feet up and down. Our job was to clear the trail from winter's havoc on the land. Moving branches, trees, and debris opened up the trail for those who came through after us. Our teacher led us while two other rangers on an ATV, armed with chainsaws, went ahead of us. By the time we reached any blockage to our path, they were already there, assessing how to move the debris, cutting it into smaller, more manageable pieces, and giving us instructions on how to accomplish the task. This process was tedious.

People generally go on hikes to reach the summit. That was not the goal for this journey. Six hours in, the five of us were tired; one had dropped off in a field and waited there, picking flowers, alone and quiet, perfectly positioned as bear bait. Seriously, who let us do this? The rest of us were worn out as well but determined to reach the summit. Together we picked up the pace. We needed to make good time on the last leg to ensure that we reached the van before dark. Panting and thirsty, we did reach the summit together. The journey up had taken us seven or eight hours; the journey down would need to only take us three or four. It was a risk, but we made unbelievable time on the descent, running the last half-mile to the car, doing whatever was necessary to reach our guides' goal and ours as well.

In my current walk with the Lord, I can think of no better imagery than this to demonstrate how he guides us. He invites us on adventures and to new places that seem a little crazy and scary. At times, he even asks us to blaze the trail for others. When he does, the first thing we need to remember is that he is responsible for our safety and for whatever happens. If he's called us to it, we go in obedience. We can trust him with our lives in security and in threat. He will never let us down.

When we're starting out, when we're training in new territory, he provides well-equipped people to help clear the way for us. And for each of us, he's appointed a guide, the Holy Spirit, who is our map.

Cling to these truths when you're blazing the trail. How foolish it would have been for those guides to assume or tell us that the path ahead wouldn't be difficult, that we wouldn't face roadblocks or treacherous terrain. They told us that the trail—not the summit—was the goal. Our sole purpose was to forge a path for others. If they had not told us what lay ahead, they wouldn't have prepared us well but would have instead deceived us.

Friend, we can trust that Jesus never ever lies to us or deceives us about the journey. We often just choose to hear what we want to hear. When we do choose to listen, he'll prepare us for difficulties. When we face the future prepared, he'll make sure we have time for the view from the summit too. He's just that good.

The way with him is not easy, but it is simple. The best adventures are like that. You take little with you, traverse tough terrain, and go on long plane rides to see something you've never seen before, perhaps something no one has seen before. You want every single thing you bring with you to have a purpose. You don't want to waste a single bit of space in your luggage. You also don't want to lug along a bunch of stuff you don't need. You don't want any extras weighing you down. Even if you really love it, you won't love it after you have to carry it for very long.

So it was, as I began writing this book, it started to feel heavy for reasons I couldn't understand.

Jesus told us as his disciples not to bring anything with us in our journey to do what he did. He doesn't want anything getting in the way of how he wants to use us. He wants us to know that he'll supply it all. He doesn't want anything to inhibit us from going and doing what he's called us to go and do.

When I was in college, a dear friend and I took two classes as part of a summer study program abroad in Spain. We decided to leave three weeks early so that the two of us could backpack through Europe together. This was before cell phones, before the movie, *Taken*, before 9/11. Our parents were totally cool with this adventure. And we were completely darling in our ignorance of the possible dangers that lurked in every country. When we went to Germany, we visited the Haufbrahaus in Munich. I thought the beer steins were so memorable and cool that I packed two in our very full backpacks to lug through the rest of Europe until I got home seven weeks later. These bad boys were ginormous. Even though they were empty, they weighed, I am certain, fifty-five pounds each. By the time I got to Switzerland, I was angry at the steins I first thought were so cute. When we reached our second stop in Italy, I downright hated them and myself for buying them.

Just a couple of months before I started writing this story, my friend Julie prayed for me at Bible study. I was wrestling with doubts and fear about the adventure Jesus was inviting me on. Comfort was holding me back. What I couldn't fathom about God was holding me back. What I had forgotten about him was holding me back. As she prayed, her words were more profound than she knew:

"Tired, tired, tired is what I heard as you spoke about doubt, fear, and feeling ill-equipped. As you spoke about rest, I saw an image of what happens when our kids fall asleep. They get really heavy. Whenever they get heavy, they drop their toys. You can drop those toys you're holding in your hands, all the things you think will equip you, and rest on him."

I needed to unpack some German steins.

I proceeded to pray after that word of revelation given to me by the power of the Holy Spirit, realizing that God was asking me to join him in a new place, a new adventure, one void of striving. I heard something so clearly unlike anything he has said before. It was bold and authoritative, and it rewrote my story once more, causing me to rely on him in a deeper way.

"Erin, I didn't choose you because of your sin or because it would make a better story. I chose you in spite of your sin, regardless of your sin. Erin, I chose you *sooooo long ago!*"

**"Erin, I didn't choose you because of your sin or because it would make a better story. I chose you in spite of your sin, regardless of your sin. Erin, I chose you sooooo long ago!"**

As I've come to agree with those words of promise and blessed assurance, I have seen even the most insignificant threads of my life weave more and more into an unbelievable and beautiful tapestry. Not a thing about me or you is wasted with God. Not even my unbelief. In fact, he used it to strengthen my faith.

Three days later, while my author friend, Chuck Ammons (go buy his book, *Life in the Overflow*, immediately!), was praying for me and encouraging me to write, he had another similar word for me. "Erin, like John, you are the disciple who Jesus loves. And I can see you reclining next to him like John did at the Last Supper."

I wanted to learn more about how John could feel so comfortable reclining next to Jesus. I went to my Bible. He was so confident in his relationship with God that he could rest in and near and on Jesus. Throughout the gospels, we see John asking Jesus bold questions, and in his New Testament Scriptures, he continues to challenge God's people with thought-provoking questions, powerful visions, and courageous examples of faith. God was not surprised by John's candor. And instead of rolling his eyes or cursing what is so profoundly unique about John, he calls forth more of those qualities from him.

In Mark 3:17, Jesus refers to John and his brother James as "sons of thunder," which the *Ellicott's Commentary for English Readers* notes is likely indicative of their disposition.[21]

Well, let's just shout hallelujah to that, shall we? The unique disposition of John launched him as a pioneer of the gospel message. Please remember, friends, Jesus doesn't want to smother your personality or your unique voice. He wants you to use it to proclaim his good news! John was a pillar of faith and challenged the church to use their individuality to advance the kingdom of God! John's bold, courageous voice was especially necessary because the disciples had been commanded not to speak after the resurrection of Jesus even though that directly opposed what Christ commanded them to do before he ascended to heaven.

What is a son of thunder to do with these two polarizing commands?

In Acts 4:20, true to his nature, John boldly proclaims, "As for us, we cannot help speaking about what we have seen and heard" (NIV).

And that was the last time I told God no. Once more, God had used my discomfort to transform me for his good purposes. (See Psalm 15:4–5.) Unburdened and at rest, I was free to write and become more of who God says I am.

Over these twelve years, as I've continued to live this out—this surrendered life, crazy-on-fire life, just-try-to-shut-me-up life—all those desires that were deep in my heart were seen by God. And I'm not talking about cars, a successful business, big houses, or huge bank accounts; rather, I'm talking about a marriage that serves God and each other, children who love the Lord and desire to hear his voice, opportunities to use my gifts for him, wisdom, and freedom. He has given us abundantly more than we could think or ask.

In moments like these, when I'm trying to comprehend all that he's done, when it's so overwhelming that I get weepy and can hardly speak because I can't understand why he would do this for me, I pray a particularly personal and powerful verse. I'll use it to share one final story with you.

King David, in all the ways he got it right with the Lord, found himself in a terrible state. He had broken all God's commands, including murder, adultery, lying, and jealousy. In his humility and fear of the Lord, he knelt before the altar of God and begged for mercy. The Lord forgave David and gave Nathan, the prophet, a vision for him of a lasting legacy.

After hearing this word, David wept and sang a song of thanksgiving, overwhelmed by God's favor and love, not just for him, but the redemption of his family. Here is a portion of his response:

"Then King David went in and sat before the LORD and prayed, 'Who am I, O Sovereign LORD, and what is my family, that you have brought me this far? And now, Sovereign LORD, in addition to everything else, you speak of giving your servant a lasting dynasty! Do you deal with everyone this way, O Sovereign LORD?'" (2 Samuel 7:18–19 NIV).

I have prayed this with each child that I've birthed, with each person I've baptized or led to salvation, with each person who has been healed or set free because of the story written in me. With each echo of this verse, the Lord reminds me of his great love.

To answer King David's question: Yes. The Lord deals with everyone with mercy and sovereignty. The same way he has dealt love and peace and patience to me, he will deal it to you as well. The same things he's done for me, he also desires for you. You are not outside the reach of his mercy. If I wasn't, you aren't. Mickey and I shouldn't have made it this far. No way. We shouldn't have the life we have or the children we've been given. The God who gave us all this in spite of ourselves, that's the God we must get to know, that's the God we have to share. He's not void of justice; he weaves mercy through his justness. I certainly can't take any credit for all that our family has been given. He brought us here; it's all his.

Mickey and I, together and separately, have had many moments of repentance and surrender. Just in writing this, the Lord worked on us in a whole new way. Thank you, Jesus! The process of healing and restoration and repentance happens over time. So be kind to yourself. I'm grateful to tell you that through all the healing, we have remained devoted and faithful to each other and the Lord through our entire marriage. Honestly, not a single moment of indiscretion.

Jesus changed me. He changed my life.

Mickey and I often say that we can't believe that was us, living the way we were. It doesn't seem like us. I'm so thankful for that. I pray that each day, we would look a little more like Jesus and a little less like ourselves. I pray that's what you see when you see us too. When you read or hear our story, I pray you see him. I pray that all that I do will bring him praise and honor and glory, for he has done great things and is worthy of all praise!

To echo King David's question, Who am I? Well, I finally know. I only know who I am because I know *whose* I am. I know it deep in my heart. I know it in my mind, and my actions—mostly, I hope—prove it. I am his daughter, Erin. I am loved. I am his child. I am blessed. I am highly favored and known by him. I could never do anything to earn that, but I want to join him in every adventure because of it!

My dear friend—we can call each other that now because you've stayed with me to the end—he is screaming the same message to you! Will you hear it? Will you receive his scandalous grace? Will you embrace your new identity? Will you believe it? Will you share it? Because you. Are. Invited.

## LET'S REFLECT:

What is the story that is stirring in your heart after reading this? How has Jesus changed you?

Who could you tell about the marvelous things he has done?

# ACKNOWLEDGMENTS

One of my favorite parts of a book is the acknowledgments. I love reading the thankfulness in the author's heart. I'm kneeling in gratitude at the feet of the following folks who joined me in this adventure.

**God the Father, God the Son, God the Holy Spirit:** Remember those ten lepers you healed and only one came back to say thank you? May I spend the rest of my life coming back to your feet to thank you for my healing. You have given me more than I deserve. You never relented in your pursuit of my heart. Now you have it. I'm all yours. I'll go anywhere with you.

**Mickey:** My words will fall flat here. You've never stopped encouraging me to run after the dreams God has placed in my heart even when it has meant pausing some of your own. Your love prepped my heart to receive God's. His love prepped my heart to receive yours. I feel heaven when I embrace your love.

**My girls:** You are teaching me how to love and trust by how you love and trust me. You've championed words you don't even understand yet. I'm so proud to be your mom. My loves, in every godly way, where I walk, may you run.

**Lisa, my editor:** What a gift you've been through this process. You brought more than commas and rephrasing skills; you brought friendship, encouragement, and hope when I was ready to scrap my words. You're a fierce woman of God! I am stronger for knowing you.

**Jeff, my graphic designer:** You're a hero! I didn't know what the cover would look like, but you saw something I couldn't see. I'm so grateful for your vision. It was such an honor to work with someone with your patience and creativity. I'm so proud of what developed with you.

**Mom and Dad:** For reading this book, crying through it, and blessing me to share it. These stories are yours too. You had a front row seat to a show you didn't want to attend. But you stayed and prayed. I don't have the words to thank you for that. I'm here because of you.

**Ruthie, Sarah, and Jason:** My whole life would be lame without you. You three were the first ones who taught me how to love and be loved. You're still my first choice of who to hang with. Your encouraging GIFs, memes, texts, and phone calls got me through this crazy journey with joy. I'm thankful God gave me you for a million reasons.

**Pop-pop and Grammy:** I cried today when you called to come and pick up the kids so that I could finish one last call with the editor. You've rescued us a million times during this process in a million ways you don't even realize. Thank you for being who you are .

**In-laws, nieces, and nephews:** This family you're in is filled with craziness, imperfection, and mad amounts of grace. I'm thankful you lean into it. Thank you for being you and keeping my kids busy while I wrote. Now, let's have a popcorn fight/dance party!

**Niki and Mariangel:** You two have been on this journey with me more than nearly anyone else. Your voices of truth and honor were in my ears as I wrote these words. I am better because of them.

**Best friend, Amber:** Your reaction to this process has been my favorite, because it's been mine: shock and awe. Because we both know deep down, we're still just two little girls who sometimes pretend to throw up in stores just to gross people out.

**My tribe of ladies:** I don't know how I became so blessed to find so many women who are strong, courageous, sensitive, faithful, smart, and funny. You huddled around me and this book. You were the relief I needed on trying days. Women's friendship should always look like this. My tears over this book were real. You saw each one, and you said, "Keep going!" I love you for that.

**Len and Robin:** You're incredible mentors and friends. Robin, you read this book before it was polished while in the middle of completing your doctoral program. You're my hero. This book is better because your eyes were on these words. Pastor Len, only heaven knows how many times you prayed for me and this book. You're the real deal, a trustworthy pastor and friend. Every church should have a faithful pastor like you.

**Chuck and Jill:** You're the first church folks Mickey and I trusted with this story. Your love, friendship, prayers, and counsel have launched this book. Jill, you are the epitome of beauty, loving others the way Jesus does. Pastor Chuck, you used your voice and influence to elevate mine. I am so grateful.

**Chris and Julie:** I love people who love to laugh. You are my people. You also make me cry. Who finds a pin that says "Best Seller" and gives it to an aspiring author? You guys. I ruined my mascara! What an emotional day, thanks to you.

**Overflow Church Staff and Members:** There are a thousand churches in our area, but I choose you. You're quirky and real, supportive and faithful. You hunger and thirst for more of Jesus. Thank you for every prayer and high-five on this journey. As far as I'm concerned, you all are as good as it gets.

**Kickstarter Donors:** You donated because you believe in the power of grace. You want to see that message released in people. You deserve to be recognized. I see you and have prayed for you. I speak blessing over you: joy, peace, love, security, prosperity, mercy, healing, and forgiveness. I thank you so very much for believing in what you couldn't yet see. These rock stars of faith are: Sarah, Corie, Kristen, Lisa, Graziella, Jasmin, Debi, Luke, Jessica, Diane, Karen, Noelle, Sara, Jami, Niki, Kaitland, Liza, Christine, Mariangel, Vicki, Ellen, Anessa, Valley's End, Geri, Laura, Ruth, Angel, Jill, Nancy, Kathy, Pat, Michael, Kathie, Jason, Mary Beth, Haley, Christina, Julie, Delia, Bob and Dawn, Paige, Wanda, Alisha, Kristin, Amber, Amy, Erin, Bryant, Ryan, and Alison.

# ENDNOTES

1  *Oxford Dictionaries*, s.v. "scandalous, (adj.)," accessed January 31, 2019, https://en.oxforddictionaries.com/definition/scandalous.

2  Jim Gascione, "Relationship Attachment Model (RAM)," *Codependency No More*, June 22, 2015, https://www.codependencynomore.com/session16/.

3  C.S. Lewis, *The Screwtape Letters*, (London: The Centenary Press, 1942), p. 70.

4  A. W. Tozer, *The Purpose of Man*, (Minnesota: Bethany House Publishing, 2009), p. 44.

5  Reference notes for John 4:6–8, *The Passion Translation Bible*, BibleGateway.com, 2017, accessed January 31, 2019, https://www.biblegateway.com/passage/?search=john+4%3A6&version=TPT.

6  C. S. Lewis, *Mere Christianity*, (New York: Macmillan Publishing Co., 1756), 107.

7  *BlueLetterBible*, "Strong's G5368," accessed January 31, 2019, https://www.blueletterbible.org/lang/lexicon/lexicon.cfm?t=kjv&strongs=g5368.

8  Ibid.

9  C. S. Lewis, *The Screwtape Letters*, 39.

10 Summary of the movie is the author's paraphrase.

11 Reference notes for Matthew 5:3, *The Passion Translation Bible*, BibleGateway.com, 2017, accessed January 31, 2019, https://www.biblegateway.com/passage/?search=matthew+5%3A3&version=TPT.

12 Oswald Chambers, *Studies in the Sermon on the Mount*, (Grand Rapids: Discovery House, 1996), 11.

13 Jim Gaffigan, *Dad Is Fat*, (New York City: Three Rivers Press, 2014), 60.

14 Staff, "Biblical Riot at Ephesus: The Archaeological Context," *Biblical Archeology*, accessed January 31, 2019, https://www.biblicalarchaeology.org/daily/biblical-sites-places/biblical-archaeology-places/biblical-riot-at-ephesus/.

15 Katrina B. Olds, *Forging The Past: Invented Histories in Counter-Reformation Spain*, (Yale: Yale University Press, 2015), 119.

16 *BlueLetterBible*, "Strong's H5828," accessed January 31, 2019, https://www.blueletterbible.org/lang/lexicon/lexicon.cfm?t=kjv&strongs=h5828.

17 Chambers, *Studies in the Sermon on the Mount*, 61.

18 Lewis, *The Screwtape Letters*, 37.

19 Lewis, *The Screwtape Letters*, 65.

20 Leonard Ravenhill, *Why Revival Tarries*, (Michigan: Bethany House Publishers, 2004), 71.

21 *Ellicott's Commentary for English Readers*, Mark 3, Biblehub.com, accessed January 31, 2019, https://biblehub.com/commentaries/ellicott/mark/3.htm.

To learn more about Erin Arruda and schedule
a speaking engagement, visit her website.

www.**erin-arruda**.com

Made in the USA
Monee, IL
16 November 2020